NEW LAWS EFFECTIVE JANUARY 1, 1996 AFFECTING CALIFORNIA COMMON INTEREST DEVELOPMENTS

COMMON INTEREST OPEN MEETING LAW (AB 46). A *meeting* is defined as any gathering of directors where at least a majority of board members are present to discuss association business. Common interest development associations must notify homeowner members of the time and place of meetings if not specified in the bylaws. Notice may be given by posting or newsletter. Emergency meetings may be called without notice to homeowners. (Amends Civil Code section 1363; adds section 1363.05.)

NOTICE OF LAWSUITS TO OWNERS (AB 463). To the extent that reserve funds are used for construction defect litigation (or borrowed for any other purpose) and a special assessment is needed to pay those funds back, homeowner approval would be needed to levy the special assessment. The new law also provides for notice to be distributed to homeowners of an association's intention to file a construction defect lawsuit against the developer not less than 30 days before filing. The notice is to specify 1) that a meeting will take place to discuss the problems, 2) the options available to the association, and 3) the time and place of the meeting. No action need be taken at this meeting. If there is a statute of limitations that would run during the 30 days before filing, then the notice would be acceptable if sent within 30 days after filing the lawsuit. (Amends Civil Code section 1365.5; adds section 1368.4.)

PRE-LITIGATION NEGOTIATION PROCESS NOW REQUIRED FOR CONSTRUCTION DEFECTS CASES (SB 1029). Before a common interest development may file a construction defect lawsuit, the developer must be given an opportunity to do testing (including destructive testing) on the property to determine the nature and extent of the defect and to try to negotiate a settlement. Previously, settlement negotiations typically took place *following* the filing of the lawsuit and could include, in addition to the developer, subcontractors. This law operates in conjunction with the "Notice of Lawsuits to Owners" law above. (Adds Civil Code section 1375)

DELETION OF DIRECTORS AND OFFICERS INSURANCE REQUIREMENT (SB 300). The requirement that associations maintain certain minimum levels of both liability and directors and officers (D&O) insurance in order to protect individual property owners from being sued for common area accidents has been changed. After January 1, 1996 the requirement for D&O coverage is deleted but association liability insurance is still required for protection. The law applies to developments with common areas owned by tenants-in-common (typically, condominiums). When the common area is owned by the association (typically, planned unit developments) the law does not apply. The requirements for disclosing information concerning association insurance to homeowners have been changed and are now more comprehensive. (Amends Civil Code sections 1365, 1365.9 and 1368.)

SATELLITE DISH ANTENNAS (AB 104). The bill prohibits community associations and others with deed restrictions against satellite dishes from enforcing them strictly. Associations may still limit satellite dishes that are over 36 inches in diameter. The association may control placement and installation, and removal costs of 36-inch and smaller dish antennas. Maintenance of the affected portion of a commonly-owned structure may be at the expense of the antenna owner. Architectural standards still apply. Owners must have association approval for the installation but the association may not unduly delay approval and may set standards for installations. (Adds Civil Code section 1376.)

NOTE

This summary of laws is not meant to be taken as inclusive of all aspects of new legislation but merely to alert readers to their existence. For guidance on the full technical requirements of these laws consult your community association attorney.

Finding the Key to Your Castle

A Guide to Cooperative Living in
Your Condominium, Townhouse
or Planned Development Home

by
Beth A. Grimm, Esq.
and
Jim R. Lane

ISBN 0-9648117-0-7

Published by
Beth A. Grimm, Esq. and Jim R. Lane

This book is designed to provide information in regard to the subject matter covered. It is provided with the understanding that the publisher and authors are not intending to render legal, accounting or other professional advice through this book. If legal or other expert assistance is required, the services of a competent professional should be sought.

Every effort has been made to make this book as interesting and helpful as possible for a general understanding of common interest development life. This is only a general guide and not the ultimate source of common interest development information.

The purpose of this book is to educate and entertain, we hope you enjoy it.

ACKNOWLEDGMENT

The authors extend thanks to those who have contributed to this project and to our families for their unflagging support and understanding.

SPECIAL ACKNOWLEDGMENT
By Beth A. Grimm

I gratefully acknowledge the wonderful community association managers I met very early on in PCAM classes, Ted Throndson, Bob Hickey and Chris Johnson; my mentors, Jim Lingl and Carole Murphy; and my many friends in CLAC, with whom I have worked side by side for years watchdogging Sacramento and helping the people who live in and manage common interest developments. Special thanks to my collaborator in this book, Jim Lane, for his gentle prodding along the way, without which this project probably would not have come to fruition this century. These and all the people I've met with, worked with, and helped through shared knowledge, brainstorming and networking have inspired me to continue practicing law exclusively in this field, to write, teach, mediate and continue to study the psychology of community association living.

DEDICATION

This book is dedicated to the selfless volunteers in the common interest development industry who contribute time and treasure to the noble cause of homeowner education; to the homeowners who serve as volunteers for the benefit of their communities; and to the many organizations dedicated to making the community association concept a working reality.

CONTENTS

Foreword i

Chapter 1   Getting Clear on the Concept   1

PART 1   Cooperative Living

Chapter 2   Rights and Responsibilities   17

Chapter 3   Rules and Reasons   31

Chapter 4   Rights, Wrongs and Expectations   51

Chapter 5   What To Do When You Don't Like It . .   67

Chapter 6   Alternative Dispute Resolution   81

PART 2   The Money Angle

Chapter 7   Dues and Don'ts   95

Chapter 8   Paying For The Unexpected   117

Chapter 9   Insurance   129

PART 3   Running the Ranch

Chapter 10   Association Management   143

Chapter 11   The Role of Volunteers   159

PART 4   For Non-owners and Nonresident Owners

Chapter 12   Renting a Condominium   173

Afterword   187
Glossary of Terms   191
Appendix   195
About the Authors   199

Backward Harry arrived at the Fracas Falls Homeowner Association annual meeting directly from dress rehearsal for a musical.

FOREWORD

FINDING THE KEY TO YOUR CASTLE

THE PARABLE OF BACKWARD HARRY

Getting things backward seemed normal to Harry. He'd done it since, as a child, he had read *Green Eggs and Ham* and couldn't fathom why his father ate ham and eggs rather than eggs and ham. Other children put on shoes and socks. Not Harry, for him it was socks and shoes; since socks went on his feet first it seemed logical. He grew up looking at life logically and making few friends. Children called him weird, threw rocks at him and pointed. Harry was undeterred and grew up as himself.

When he was old enough he voted for the best candidate, not caring about political party affiliation. Who could be right all the time? he asked people in his logical way, conceding that he could make a mistake too. Going to work from home Harry traveled forth and back over dale and hill and eventually earned enough as a dance and song man to buy a condominium at the Fracas Falls complex.

At the annual meeting of Fracas Falls Homeowners Association, the first since Harry moved in, one owner after another stood to express unhappiness because they felt the manager or board of directors had trod upon their *inalienable* rights.

"I demand my *inalienable* right to raise goats in my back yard," said one homeowner who had three goats and carried an aroma about him that kept others from shaking his hand.

"And I," interjected another, "demand my *inalienable* right to park my collection of classic Yugos in guest parking."

A third homeowner arose. "I demand my *inalienable* right to install a spa on my balcony so I can entertain my guests with a view of the city lights below. Your architectural review committee be damned."

Another arose and shouted angrily, "What does *inalienable* mean?"

Then the owners, with the exception of Harry, rose as one and chorused, "Our home is our castle. We can do what we want. It's a free country! Who do you think you are? We *have* a Constitution, you know."

As one, with the exception of Harry, they sat down heavily in their chairs, arms crossed, jaws set tightly, glaring at the board of directors (now reduced to a bare quorum as the result of *another* instant resignation). In the odd silence that followed the outburst one timid voice could be heard.

"Mr. President, may I be recognized?"

It was Harry, who had come to his feet, standing with one hand raised as he had been taught in school. The president acknowledged the diminutive man while the homeowners groaned.

"Siddown, Harry," one said. Another added, "Professor Backwards is getting ready to speak, let's all stand on our heads." Still another spoke, "Whatever you have to say, we ain't interested, you geek."

Having come to the meeting directly from dress rehearsal for a musical, Harry still wore tap shoes with white spats, a large-checkered jacket with wide shoulders, and a straw skimmer. He could have been mistaken for a court jester, had the shoes been more pointy. His garb made him even more clown-like among the casually dressed homeowners. Harry, accustomed to performing before audiences, nonetheless felt trepidation wash over him as he stood in front of the mocking mob. With the slightest waver in his voice he began, "Mr. President, I demand my responsibilities." The board members looked perplexed—was this some kind of a joke?

The homeowners hooted and flung invectives at the dance and song man who had come to their meeting. When the room finally quieted and the only noise was residual chuckling from one member who always caught on late, Harry spoke again, now with more determination, his trepidation beginning to fade.

"The reason I am demanding my responsibilities is that I have to get them taken care of before I can even think about rights, let alone *inalienable* rights. I guess that everyone else here has already taken care of their responsibilities or they wouldn't be demanding their rights."

Now, with thumbs hooking his suspenders and his left foot softly tapping a time step, he continued: "So, Mr. President, I demand that the board accept me as a volunteer. The Means and Ways Committee might be able to use my help. I demand of myself the responsibility for cleaning out my garage so I can park my car inside and not in guest parking. I demand that I pay my monthly assessment by the first and not wait until the sixteenth then complain about the late charge." Booming toward a big finish—after all, he *was* an actor—he declared: "I **demand** that I keep in mind what John Kennedy said:

'Our privileges can be no greater than our obligations. The protection of our rights can endure no longer than the performance of our responsibilities.'"

When Backward Harry had finished the room remained silent for long seconds. Even his left foot was still. There was before him a sea of bobbing heads as the full impact of Harry's words sunk in.

Slowly, the goat farmer arose and turned to the audience who, as one, leaned away. "I always made fun of Harry because he got things backward. But he has made me see things differently. I see now that Harry is a dangerous man, a fool who could ruin everything." From one of his pockets he withdrew a fistful of goat chow and threw it in Harry's face.

The audience, whose heads had been bobbing in unison a moment before, arose (yes, as one) and following suit—the most cooperation anyone had seen among them in years—pummeled Harry with Styrofoam coffee cups, half-eaten bagels and several dozen fig newtons the president's wife had brought. Harry *was* a dangerous man and had to be brought down. If responsibility ahead of rights caught on, there was no telling what might happen at Fracas Falls.

Harry's point is the point and purpose of this book. A balance of rights and responsibilities—privileges and obligations—is necessary for people to live successfully in a condominium or planned development. Balance is achievable only when everyone involved understands or, at least accepts, the organization to which they will belong as paying members.

At Fracas Falls the scales had tipped dangerously toward rights and away from responsibilities—just as we find happening all too often in modern society. In this case, the scale was close to toppling completely. Already the word had gotten around real estate circles that it was near impossible to sell Fracas Falls units because the complex showed so poorly. With goats in one back yard, with their odor and constant braying; the guest parking filled with old Yugos in various states of decay; and the balcony sagging with the weight of a water-wasting spa, there were more than enough turn-offs for potential buyers. But there were still others. The grass had been worn away where children rode their bikes and the cacophony raised by Big Wheels racing around the circular drive assaulted the ears without mercy.

Harry's neighbors were angry that their property values had sunk to the bottom of the condo market. Naturally, they blamed the directors. Some had filed lawsuits against the association, a move that made potential buyers even more skittish. The board of directors, made up of homeowners, faced high turnover. There were monthly resignations. Appointments filled the vacancies but the homeowners coming forward to accept the jobs were interested not in the overall problems at Fracas Falls, but simply wanted special approvals for their own purposes: converting the attic to a guest room and adding a dormer window to the roof; installing a large revolving clothes line; plastic flamingos on the common area lawn; a wind chime collection; and a breeding kennel for llamas.

A few courageous directors were determined to reverse the trend. They were constantly vilified as they tried to put an end to bicycles on the lawns, parking in the fire lanes and speeding cars. They had difficulty reaching a quorum at board meetings, some having quit going to meetings reasoning that it was a dirty job and they did not want to do it. Who could blame them—they were doing all the dirty work—for free—taking all the blame, and losing their friends to boot.

Fracas Falls Condominiums may sound like an exaggeration but there is nothing in Harry's story that could not happen in any other association (except for maybe Harry himself). Substitute the goats for chickens or a rooster and we may be telling your story instead of Harry's. Whether a complex is allowed to degenerate into a "Fracas Falls" is entirely up to its homeowners (remember—board members are also homeowners).

This book illustrates how different forces affect homeowner associations in California. State statutes, federal law, local ordinances, utility company regulations, assessment districts, state-imposed corporate mandates, mortgage lender policies and the governing documents of the associations themselves all bear on operation of homeowner associations. But the single greatest force is the combined will of the homeowners to maintain their property values and to actively participate in (or at least grudgingly accept) cooperative living as a way of life.

In the following pages you will find references to the guiding laws and statutes should you need to do further research. Sections of the California *Civil Code* are referenced by section, e.g. (§1351), and other laws and codes are spelled out in full.

The law depicted in these chapters is current as of January 1995. Much of the information is, however, timeless. Laws will continue to change, but human nature will not. It is the melding of these two polar forces that makes living in a condominium or planned development challenging and rewarding. The authors hope you will find this book fun as well as instructive. Most of all, we hope that you all find the key to your own castle, keep it, and live happily ever after.

Your Castle Guides

Stay Together and Don't Touch Anything

In this book you will stumble onto **Condoguru**, a self-assured soul who is convinced that he knows all and sees all in the common interest development arena. He was selected to respond to letters from CID residents and owners because of his unfailingly calm, respectful demeanor and because he has a hide like a rhinoceros.

Condoguru occasionally needs assistance with the finer points of law, though he would challenge that point. At these moments, as though through prestidigitation, the Explainer of Law for Common Interest Developments —or as she is known among peers, **El Cid**—rises to the challenge as would cream seek dominance over milk or as the evanescent mists cloak clear morning mountain lakes.

CHAPTER 1

Getting Clear on the Concept

**I signed some papers in escrow called CC&Rs, but
they were too big to read and in legal *gobbledygook*.
What did I get myself into?**

B oo Boo, Dockers and Tulip are outcasts. Some would say
that these innocent felines are victims of the Lakeside Village Condominium Association CC&Rs that prohibited
four-legged pets. Others would say the association was the victim
of a stubborn owner. It took the California Supreme Court to finally evict the cats. How could three cats get such attention—three
cats that presumably knew nothing of the legal storm surrounding
their presence in a no-pets condominium?

Condominium association directors and the industry that
provides services to homeowner associations the length of California nervously awaited the fate of these animals. They knew the
outcome would either uphold the authority of these associations to
enforce reasonable restrictions on property use or declare open sea-
son on any restriction that an individual homeowner happened to
object to. Already portrayed as anti-freedom despots and worse,
volunteer directors of these associations could expect to come under increasing fire.

The dispute over Boo Boo, Dockers and Tulip (which we will revisit in detail in a later chapter), like hundreds of disputes preceding it, turned not on an interpretation of what a restriction in the CC&Rs said, but rather on whether the restriction could be enforced in the face of mitigating circumstances. If the CC&Rs prohibited pets, could a homeowner properly keep pets if no one saw, heard or smelled them?

At the core of such disagreements is this document known as the Covenants, Conditions and Restrictions—the CC&Rs. Simply put, CC&Rs are restrictions on the way land is to be used. These restrictions most often have their beginnings with the original owner of the land. In dividing it into two or more plots, the developer plans the project then writes restrictions on the use of the property to keep the development operating and looking much the way it was set up. Two or more owners who were not the original developers can also agree to these sorts of use restrictions for their adjacent plots of land. Neighbors can draw up CC&Rs to provide for road or bridge maintenance.

Once these restrictions are properly recorded they attach themselves to the land and stay there, even when the land is bought and sold. The restrictions can be changed or terminated only if a sufficient number of affected owners agree, according to the amendment clause that most CC&Rs have. So the CC&Rs are stuck to the land and everything on it like crazy glue. When a plan of development is also properly filed the land and project become a common interest development (CID).

The CC&Rs are often referred to as a contract. This comes from the fact that when people buy into these developments, they are considered to have legally consented or agreed to accept the CC&Rs even if they don't specifically know about them.

KEY POINT
Once the CC&Rs are
properly recorded they attach
themselves to the land and stay
attached even when the land is
bought and sold.

The CC&Rs are recorded with the local county recorder's office when the development is created. They show up on title reports as restrictions on the land, and if the transaction is properly done they are most generally noted by some reference on the new owner's deed. Each new owner in a CID inherits the rights and obligations of the prior owner.

A homeowner association is created through specific CC&R language put there by the property developer. The association is responsible for managing both the property and the money collected for its maintenance. The association and all owners have rights, restrictions and obligations flowing from the CC&Rs.

The CID concept of shared ownership dates far back in time. Frequently marketed these days as *carefree living*, CID life is more accurately described as *cooperative living*. Owners share amenities that would be prohibitively expensive for individuals to purchase on their own and contribute to maintenance of those amenities and their homes through assessments collected by a homeowner association. To have use of a swimming pool, spa, tennis courts, horse trails, docks, clubhouse and other recreational facilities without shouldering the entire expense appeals to many people. More than thirty million people in the United States have been attracted by the benefits offered by this form of homeownership and the number is growing.

California CIDs are specifically addressed and defined in *The Davis-Stirling Common Interest Development Act (Civil Code* sections [§§] 1350 through 1374). CIDs come in several forms: condominiums, planned unit developments, stock cooperatives and community apartment projects. By far, condominiums (or "condos") are the most popular form, comprising about three-quarters of California CIDs. Planned unit developments, (or PUDs) make up about one-quarter of the CIDs. The other two forms, stock cooperatives and community apartment projects, make up a very small percentage of the total. In a community apartment project an owner shares interest in the land and has an exclusive right to occupy one of the apartments. A stock cooperative, in the CID context, is a corporation that owns title to the buildings and land. The shareholder has a right to live in a unit in the building but does not actually own any portion of the building or grounds. Stock cooperatives and community apartments won't be specifically addressed in this book though they are governed by the same laws as condos and PUDs.

Condominiums

"You mean I just mortgaged myself for thirty years for *airspace*?"

This concept is a little difficult to grasp or to accept because of a long history of pride in American *land* ownership. Americans want to own *dirt*. When there's a building on that *dirt*, Americans want to own it all. They want to be "king" of their castle (although there are few authentic castles in the U.S.). It's a *power/pride* thing. A cube of airspace is elusive—hard to hang onto, hard to see, hard to *grasp* mentally. Dirt, you can stand on it, see it, survey it, fence it, plow it, let it run through your fingers or make a mud pie of it.

Rules and restrictions on the use of one's *real* property are another concept that is somewhat difficult to accept. However, all property owners are subject to limits on their land. There are local zoning and use restrictions on nuisances, noise, parking of vehicles, visible garbage and trash, setbacks and building codes. Those who rent or lease are subject to any number of limitations which might include bans on pets, barbecues, second floor waterbeds, loud music, restrictions on backing into parking stalls, dilapidated cars or auto repair on the premises, parking in the visitor spaces and penalties for forgetting to pay rent on time. It's called "living in society." Hermits and nonconformists get along better in the mountains.

If we bristle at the way our lives are controlled by the landlords of the world, why would we buy into a condominium association where many of the rules look the same as those at an apartment building? *Home ownership*—it's that simple!

Home ownership brings to mind cottages and picket fences. Why, if we could afford a single family home, would we choose a condo instead? Maybe it's the beauty of *no* lawn mowing, *no* pool cleaning, *no* tree trimming, *no* painting or *no* pulling weeds. Maybe its the *safety* of a gated community, an affordable *view* home, the recreational *amenities,* the community atmosphere, or the opportunity to *serve* on a community board. Maybe its just simple fiscal reality—for many it's the *only affordable way to achieve status as an American homeowner.* Has anyone ever said, "I'm a homeowner," without their pride showing through? It's the American dream, and common interest developments represent fulfillment of that dream for millions of Americans. So where's the hitch? In later chapters we will explore the hitches, but first it helps to understand the condominium concept a little more clearly.

What You Own in a Condo

In a *condominium project* (which is defined in *Civil Code* §1351(f)), ownership of most of the development is held jointly by all the owners. The living quarters are called *units* which are located in buildings making up part of the *common area*. While an owner purchases a particular *unit*, he or she actually holds title to the airspace within the four walls that is exclusively his or her property *and* a share of the *common area* as tenant-in-common with all of the other unit owners. Sometimes an owner will also possess a balcony, parking space, deck, garage or carport along with the other property described.

KEY POINT
A condominium owner has title to the air space inside his or her unit and a pro rata or equal share in the common area with the rest of the unit owners.

Items of ownership are designated on the original plan of development (described in more detail below) as well as in the deed given to the owner when the property is purchased. What follows is a more detailed description of the types of property in a condominium development.

Common Area. This is the entire condominium complex except for the *separate interests* known as *units*. Common area includes the structures, grounds, and amenities. All unit owners hold title to their separate interest plus a share of the common area as *tenants-in-common*.

Exclusive Use or Restricted Common Areas. These are portions of the common area that are specified for use by one or more but fewer than all the members, such as the decks, balconies, patios and garages. If designated on the condo plan or deed as belonging with a particular unit and on the deed description, the owner holds *title* to these areas. If not, the ownership question is a little more iffy. Commonly, back yards, front porches, exterior doors, patio or yard dividing fences, windows and other such items and spaces are considered *exclusive use* areas. They may be designated in the condo plan, the CC&Rs, or the deed, or not designated at all. *Civil Code* §1351(i) illustrates several examples of *exclusive use* areas and states that they are *allocated exclusively to the separate interests* but the statute does not say whether "*allocated to*" relates to ownership or use. Certain utility lines can also be designated for *exclusive use*. Ownership and control of these areas as they relate to maintenance and liability exposure will be discussed in later chapters.

Separate Interest. This is the *castle* part of the equation— yours as far as the eye can see when the drapes are drawn. This is *your* space. You actually own the interior surface of the wall *inward* and whatever is located within this *inward space.* This could include a furnace, water heater, or air conditioner, and does include the shower or bathtub and the built-in cabinets and the closet doors.

Planned Unit Developments

A *planned unit development (PUD),* or *planned development*, as it is called by *Civil Code* §1353(k), often bears great similarity to a traditional neighborhood. It may consist of connected residential buildings such as duplexes or fourplexes or it can be entirely separate, stand-alone residences, each on several acres. Sometimes they are called townhouses. Each owner owns a *lot* (some real *dirt*) upon which the home sits. What makes it a CID is that an association has been formed that governs, primarily, the architectural aspects of the homes and community, the uses allowed, and any common area amenities such as a neighborhood pool and clubhouse, open space parks, equestrian trails, tennis courts, boat docks or other recreational amenities. The association generally holds title to the *lots* or parcels upon which the *amenities* are located which is different than the tenancy-in-common ownership of a condominium project. The CID may be formed even without common areas. The association might have maintenance or insurance responsibilities with rights of entry to or through the lots and structures. It generally has the right to collect assessments and lien the properties when the assessments are not paid.

KEY POINT

An owner in a PUD holds title to the land under his home and the building and also shares in ownership of the common area, but this comes through his membership in the association and not as a tenant-in-common with other homeowners.

What Owns You

The Association. (Cue the *Jaws* music.) This is the entity in which you have become an indivisible part through your ownership of a unit or lot. In a condo complex made up of 200 separate interests (residences), you are a 1/200th owner in everything that is not your *separate interest.* Your share is *indivisible* and *inseparable* from the association, meaning that you can't take your 1/200th interest and run. You cannot paint your windows black and bar up your door to shut out the world. The other owners, members of the association, have some say in what you do in there—if it affects them, or if it is a violation of the CC&Rs. You cannot stake out your 1/200th part of the swimming pool or common area lawn for your lawn chair or picnic table and keep other people out of it. You can share your *ownership* in a separate interest. A married couple can hold joint ownership in the 1/200th share but when they are divorced, neither can split off half of the share. The couple may be divisible, but the *separate interest* is not.

The association may or may not be a corporation but the law treats all CIDs pretty much the same, at least as it relates to operations. (The differences usually become more important in regard to questions of liability.) As a nonprofit mutual benefit corporation, which is the most common organizational structure of associations in California, the condominium or planned unit development association must be guided by a board of directors. Directors are generally elected by the owners (which includes developer representatives at the early stages) and they are most often unpaid volunteers. The primary purpose of such an association (which is found in the Articles of Incorporation, if incorporated) is to *"protect and maintain the value of the property."* That is a big job—big enough to devote Part 3 of this book to it.

Corporate and Governing Documents. If you are already an owner in a CID, these are the piles of paper you were probably handed in the escrow office, which you then placed in that dresser drawer with the broken handle that doesn't open and you probably haven't missed—yet. Corporate and governing documents (which are defined in *Civil Code* §1351(j)) include the Articles of Incorporation (if incorporated) or Articles of Association, the Condominium Plan (if a condo), the CC&Rs, bylaws, rule book and any other documents that govern the operation of the association, its obligations, and rights of the association members.

Articles of Incorporation: The Articles of Incorporation are the *charter* document of the association and are filed with the Secretary of State. Their purpose is to identify the association as a corporation and establish an entity that can do business and operate under the rules and protections of the California *Corporations Code.* They set forth the purposes of the corporation which, as stated earlier, generally include preservation of property values as the primary obligation.

Condominium Plan. The condominium plan (defined in *Civil Code* §1351(e)) serves the purpose of describing the physical aspects of the development. When this plan is filed with the county recorder it becomes a public document. The architectural drawings used by the building contractors are separate from the condominium plan and are not a part of the governing corporate documents. The architectural plans and specifications are, however, an important and often overlooked reference document and should be preserved by the association. The plans show underground utility routes, drainage, building specifications and details of floor plans. This information is essential for planning projects such as reroofing or plumbing retrofits.

Subdivision Maps. These are the maps that are filed with the county recorder at the origination of the development that describe the CID as a subdivision and illustrate the lot designations for PUDs and units for the condo development.

CC&Rs (Covenants, Conditions & Restrictions). This document (which is also referred to as the "*declaration*") is created by the developer of the property to help retain the original scheme he or she had in mind. The document defines ownership interests, and sets parameters for use, construction, and authority of the owners, the developer, and the association. The rights and obligations found in the CC&Rs "run" with the property by virtue of a very important clause that is always included which makes the document applicable to *successors-in-interest, heirs, and assigns,* of the owners—anyone who might come into possession of the property.

Sometimes association drafting committees who set out to amend the CC&Rs leave this important clause out because they don't understand the extent of its impact. It is nothing less than the *legal glue* that attaches the CC&Rs to the property and to all subsequent purchasers and heirs of properties in a CID.

Often, the CC&Rs provide protections for the developer by creation of a two-class voting structure, giving the developer three votes per unit while homeowners get one vote per unit until most of the units are sold. This voting scheme is perfectly legal, protects the developer, and assures retention of control so long as he or she is still building or has interest in units in the development. The CC&Rs may contain *lender voting rights* specifying that certain provisions may not be changed or eliminated without lender consent. These clauses help the developer get the development "lender certified" so that each purchaser in the development does not have to go through a process where the development itself is evaluated for conflict with lender regulations. This document is the foremost operating tool of the association. It is the foundation for rules related to everyday living and uses of the property.

Since the CC&Rs specify acceptable building standards and uses of the property for the owners in the development, out-of-date, inapplicable, unenforceable or ambiguous CC&Rs can be worse than useless. They could be detrimental to the association and all its members by promoting friction and disputes because of conflicts with current law. Typically, the CC&Rs themselves, will list the percentage of owners needed to approve amendments to the CC&Rs.

Bylaws. Association bylaws are the organizational document that guides the board of directors in its activities. They should not be a reiteration of the CC&Rs because their purpose is different. It is essential, though, that they do *not* conflict with the CC&Rs. Bylaws generally provide standards and requirements for meetings (of the membership and board of directors) and elections, as well as officers' and directors' duties and powers.

Rule Book, Regulations and Policies. The rule book, regulations and policies flow from the CC&Rs. They are adopted by the board under authority stated in the bylaws, articles, or CC&Rs. The rules are generally aimed at simplifying and clarifying responsibilities and expectations placed on residents. The rule book should serve as a common reference for residents who are interested in how many and what kind of pets they may keep (three cats?); parking for themselves and their guests; how to register a complaint or question; the rules and hours of the spa, pool, RV park or tennis courts, etc.

Most often the directors can update the rule book without a vote of the entire membership as long as the change is legal, reflects the CC&Rs and does not exceed the authority of the board.

The Laws

Throughout this handbook you will find reference to various laws and statutes that affect condominium associations. In 1985, in the wake of numerous problems arising from haphazard management of some CIDs, the California Legislature created *The Davis-Stirling Common Interest Development Act*. It was designed to provide guidance for associations and specifically addresses some of the most troubling problems associations face. *The Davis-Stirling Act* covers items such as financial issues (budgets, reserve funds and collection of assessments), liability issues for board members and owners, and maintenance issues (as in exclusive use areas which are not specific enough in CC&Rs to be useful).

The act became effective January 1, 1986, and it contains the bulk of statutes relating to common interest developments and the rights and obligations of the associations, managing agents and homeowners in CIDs. At the time this book was published, *The Davis-Stirling Act* comprised California *Civil Code* §§1350 through 1374. New statutes are proposed annually so you can expect this body of law to keep expanding to address the needs of CIDs. In 1995 the lion's share of proposed modifications to *The Davis-Stirling Act* involved additional rights for homeowners and additional obligations on the part of the associations.

All references to sections of law in this book are to the California *Civil Code* unless otherwise stated and are identified with the symbol "§" and section number. The *Nonprofit Mutual Benefit Corporation Law*, beginning in the 7000 series of the *Corporations Code* statutes was added in 1980. These statutes more generally govern association operations involving membership and board meetings and issues related to meetings such as quorum and notice requirements and elections.

As you journey through this book you'll find references to these various laws, which do *own you* in a sense when you purchase in a common interest development that is subject to *The Davis-Stirling Act*.

Ownership in a CID is sometimes portrayed in the negative—usually as the result of misunderstandings about what a CID is and how it works. While reading this book keep in mind that the law, and CC&R restrictions in general, provide important protections that make the CID style of living, in many respects, more desirable than single family home ownership in the average city neighborhood.

CONDOGURU
SPEAKS

Q: *It seems like my association is being inconsistent. The CC&Rs say one thing but the rule book says something else. I thought the rules were supposed to reflect CC&Rs.*

CONDOGURU: I checked out your association's documents and you are right, there is an inconsistency between CC&Rs and rules. While, in theory at least, the rule book should flow like sweet nectar from the golden fount of the CC&Rs, it isn't always possible. This distressing state of affairs reflects the speed with which our Sacramento solons add laws to our lives. (According to Webster a *solon* is either a wise and skillful lawgiver or [merely] a member of a legislative body. *You decide which.*)

In addition, the courts can't escape responsibility for the rapid changes. The onslaught of rulings from judges create law by default.

CC&Rs are filed with the county as controlling documents. Altering them to conform with the annual changes in law would be an expensive process requiring legal review, homeowner approval, and refiling. So it isn't feasible to do it often. Since the CC&Rs are the key legal document governing the association they *should* be current. As a practical matter, it is nearly impossible to maintain up-to-date CC&Rs.

This being the case, association directors often look for an easier way to comply.

The association bylaws can be modified by a vote of the general membership at an annual meeting. But bylaws govern *functioning* of the association and don't address the issues of daily life that affect the actual livability of the community and owners' rights and responsibilities.

That leaves the rule book. The association directors can make changes to the rule book more easily than any other document. As long as adequate notification is given to those affected by the rules, new or changed rules that reflect the latest law can be incorporated by board vote.

So, the answer to your question is, "Yeah, so what?"

PART 1

COOPERATIVE LIVING

CHAPTER 2   RIGHTS AND RESPONSIBILITIES

CHAPTER 3   RULES AND REASONS

CHAPTER 4   RIGHTS, WRONGS AND EXPECTATIONS

CHAPTER 5   WHAT TO DO WHEN YOU DON'T LIKE IT

CHAPTER 6   ALTERNATIVE DISPUTE RESOLUTION

CHAPTER 2

Rights and Responsibilities

Look, I bought this place to get some of the carefree living that my realtor talked about. So why did I get a note that I have to fix my own garage door?

Part I—WHO FIXES WHAT IN A COMMON INTEREST DEVELOPMENT

One of the greatest sources of friction, frustration, and frazzled nerves in common interest association affairs is who is responsible for what. Many of the disagreements between owners and the CID directors occur because owners move in expecting that the board will take care of everything—*carefree living*, as advertised. After all, this is a dues-paying society and shouldn't those dues cover everything? The short answer is no.

In some cases it is clear as to who maintains what. Sure, some of the expenses are shared, but all too often the governing documents lack specifics. The proof of this is in the growing need for lawyers who deal exclusively in this type of law.

A dispute will often begin with someone declaring, "That's why I pay my dues every month—so I don't have to bother with

@#&*!" That could be true or not, depending on what the @#&*! happens to be. There are three different areas of responsibility that are divided between the association and the owners.

The first, the **common area**, is the grounds and facilities (and buildings in the case of condos) owned in common by all the association's members, or (in a PUD) owned by the association. Responsibility for the common area is clear—the association must take charge. This is one of the purposes for which members pay regular assessments (monthly dues).

The **separate interests**, as defined in Chapter 1, include the private areas comprising the owner's living space which are clearly the owner's responsibility. In a condo this area is the *unit* while in a planned development it is generally the *lot* and building upon it. Townhouses with common walls are often set up as planned developments but for maintenance obligations they are usually treated more like condos than separate residences.

Many of the disputes over maintenance responsibilities arise in regard to **exclusive use common areas** or from items not mentioned specifically in the documents (such as wiring or plumbing lines). Areas not encompassed within the unit but that are used by only one or fewer than all of the owners are **exclusive use common areas**. Patios, garage doors, balconies, outside storage room doors and front porches are typical **exclusive use common areas.**

A true common area is available for equal access and use by all association members and that is why all owners contribute to maintenance costs. However, since a patio, storage area, garage, or back yard is used *exclusively* by the occupants of a single residence who normally control access, it is common for the maintenance responsibility for those items to fall on the shoulders of that owner. By exception, there may be good reason to treat a garage, balcony or carport differently—it may well be more logical for the association to retain responsibility for maintenance in order to retain *control* over painting, structural stability, pest control or roof repairs and replacement.

"I suppose I should have read the CC&Rs—especially the part on exclusive use common area maintenance."

Plumbing repairs are often a dicey issue, especially if the work is costly or involves removal and replacement of a shower stall or drywall, or there are extensive damages caused by a water leak. Termites cause more problems than simple destruction of wood. Sometimes there is a need for complete fumigation requiring all attached units to be vacated for days. Responsibility for termite damage is often a source of heated disagreement between owners and the board of directors.

Questions to consider in sorting out responsibility in any maintenance dispute include: 1) What, if anything, do the documents say? 2) What, if anything, does the law say? 3) Is the damage in a common area or in an exclusive use common area? 4) What or who caused the problem? 5) Has this problem come up before and how was it handled then? and 6) Is there any advantage or disadvantage to the association if it unnecessarily assumes responsibility? Would the association benefit by retaining control or set an undesirable precedent? An attorney should consider all these questions before giving an opinion on who has to pay. This is where life becomes interesting for the board of directors.

From time to time homeowners are faced with some unpleasant revelations as to their responsibilities. A condo owner was surprised and unhappy to find that he was responsible, at least in part, for an underground telephone cable. The cable ran from a common area terminal, located on the side of his garage, to his residence. Even where this cable runs under common area ground, it is not the association's responsibility. This situation is specifically addressed in *The Davis-Stirling Act*. California *Civil Code* §1351 specifically includes telephone service wiring as *exclusive use common area*. Section 1364 defines responsibilities, generally, for telephone wiring. The owner's responsibility was shared equally with four of his neighbors because the phone line served only those five residences. The reason telephone cable is considered an exclusive use common area item is because it is used by, and benefits, *one or more but fewer than all* the members of the association. The residents served by that phone cable have equal responsibility for its repair. The association generally has no responsibility—however, if the association's landscaper chopped the cable in half digging a hole for a sprinkler head, the responsibility changes. That is why factors other than the documents and the law must be considered.

KEY POINT
Exclusive use common areas benefit *one or more but fewer than all* members of the association; maintenance responsibility generally resides with the homeowner using it.

Maintenance Versus Replacement

Confusion may arise over whether the work required on a unit is *maintenance* or *replacement*. Consider a simple case: an accidental fire destroys one condo unit. Most often the association's insurance will pay for replacement of the structure, but it will not pay for furnishings or personal property that was damaged. There may well be a dispute over replacement of built-in cabinets or other interior improvements added after original construction. An association would certainly not *maintain* these, but an owner might expect the association's master insurance policy to cover their *replacement* if destroyed by a fire. Now let's look at a grease fire on a kitchen range that scorches the interior walls and cupboards and ruins the curtains. The fire did no *structural* damage that would be covered by the association's fire policy. The owner is, therefore, fully responsible in this case.

In a different example, the CC&Rs might require the association to maintain the garage doors (to keep them painted, etc.) but replacement might be the owner's responsibility.

The value of all the units in a CID can be adversely affected if any single residence is poorly maintained. Even where the owner is clearly responsible, associations often have legal authority to force the owner to fix the problem. Sometimes the CC&Rs give an association the right to enter the unit after reasonable notice (or without notice in the case of an emergency) to make repairs or do maintenance. The CC&Rs should say whether the association can charge the homeowner for the work with an individual assessment. If the CC&Rs don't address collection, and the owner doesn't voluntarily pay, then the association may have to take the case to small claims (or a higher) court. An association also can sue the homeowner to get compliance under authority of *Civil Code* §1354 if an owner is refusing to perform required maintenance. Any owner can sue another owner or the association (if it is not performing maintenance) under that statute also.

Rights of entry in PUDs with detached homes are not usually as broad as in condo or townhouse developments. Since the PUD homes are individually owned and there is often space between them, they are not as likely to be directly affected by problems in poorly maintained adjacent homes. However, the type and severity of the problem may still qualify for association or neighbor intervention.

Fortunately, entering condominium and townhouse units is seldom necessary because most people want to get along, preserve their property, and respond quickly when there is a problem.

Much of the confusion about responsibilities stems from the perception that the association is the equivalent of landlord. In reality, the difference between the two is significant. The extent of powers, rights, obligations, and authority for landlords is more extreme because the landlord owns all of the property and is the ultimate controller. And the investment and motivation of the resident is much less. A renter can walk away from the rented property with little or no further responsibility. An association member has no such freedom, being more closely linked to the property through a deed of trust and rights and expectations of the mortgage holder. In a CID the new owner signs documents taking on much more responsibility than simply paying the mortgage—but few seem to remember later. By accepting the terms of sale the owner has assumed a responsibility, as did all the other owners in the development, to follow the CC&Rs. A CID homeowner fighting the CC&Rs and fighting with his association is in reality also fighting himself—especially where a lawsuit is filed. It is *his or her* assessments that pay, in part, for the association's lawyer.

With approval of the CID owners (and sometimes required approval of mortgage lenders), maintenance responsibilities can be shifted by changing the CC&Rs. Whenever CC&Rs are amended the association should use the process to clarify maintenance responsibilities so that items commonly disputed are clarified. It will help if the CC&Rs spell out responsibilities in unambiguous terms.

KEY POINT

An owner in a common interest development who sues the association is suing himself. His or her assessments are paying for the board's legal defense

Short of document amendments, which can be costly and time-consuming, the most constructive approach to resolving maintenance disputes is willing and intelligent involvement of the parties in finding a solution. Some responsibilities can be altered by a board-directed change in association policy.

In one example, an aging condominium association's CC&Rs gave responsibility for termite eradication to the home-owners. The statute that applies to termite eradication (§1364) generally attributes the responsibility to the association unless the CC&Rs state otherwise, as happens in this example. Inspections and treatments by homeowners in the absence of a coordinated plan had proved inadequate and the infestations had reached the point where fumigations would soon be needed. The board recognized that it would be virtually impossible for a homeowner trying to sell his unit to get a clean termite report since the condos were in multiunit buildings. A single unit could not be fumigated. The entire building would have to be vacated, and families would be forced into hotels for several days during fumigation. Leaving the burden on a single owner to coordinate and perhaps even pay for the entire building treatment was neither practical nor reasonable.

The directors found relief for this situation in *Civil Code* §1364, which gave the association legal authority to require all families to leave the building and to pay their own expenses while the building was fumigated. This valuable tool was unavailable to any individual owner. The assumption of control by the association proved beneficial here.

In this case, the owners in the association voted to change the CC&Rs so that the association could take control. The association hired a contractor and immediately began a program of inspection and spot treatments. This new maintenance obligation increased member dues slightly but the trade-off was better care and likely prevention of building fumigation. The association—which consists collectively of all the members together—made an intelligent move in favor of the cooperative living concept.

Part II—WHO CAN BUILD WHAT IN A COMMON INTEREST DEVELOPMENT

I want to install one of those electric garage doors that folds up when it closes, but my neighbor tells me I have to get approval from the association—*que pasa*?

Generally, exterior, structural, or visible modifications to a unit or separate interest can't be done until approved by an architectural committee or the board of directors. There are at least three aspects to consider when someone wants to modify his or her dwelling: maintenance, structure and aesthetics. Anything that affects the roofs (installing skylights, solar panels, etc.) or structures (moving beams or knocking down walls) requires approval. Sometimes associations develop and distribute guidelines ahead of time for skylights, solar installations, private gardens or trellises, fence types, exterior colors, screen doors, etc., so that owners will be guided in an acceptable direction as they make their plans.

Architectural guidelines are helpful to the owners since there may be considerable expense involved in developing architectural drawings and plans. It's reasonable and efficient for them to know ahead of time what might be acceptable—and it may head off a dispute later. Guidelines encourage modifications that are consistent with acceptable standards. If a requested change falls within the association's architectural guidelines then the change will generally be approved. Conditions may be placed on the construction method, the improvement itself, the timing, acceptance of liability and maintenance of the improvement.

Consistency in *look* and *feel* is one of the biggest selling points in a CID. Proposed improvements that are harmonious and aesthetically pleasing are generally acceptable unless the modification infringes on the common area, violates a setback, causes additional maintenance or liability for the association, blocks another resident's view, or interferes with another's quiet enjoyment of his property.

Disputes generally arise when someone has made, or threatens to make, a change without seeking approval or when the change is in violation of the CC&Rs or existing standards. Sometimes one owner learns that another has installed a nonconforming structure or improvement that is not readily obvious to the casual passerby, and lodges a complaint with the association. This usually occurs when the two neighbors don't care for each other. Some violations are discovered by the manager or board members during property inspections. The violations aren't crimes. They are, however, *illegal* in a manner of speaking. Owners with the *castle mentality* argue that they should be able to add on whatever they like without regard for others. Associations that are consistent in pursuing violations of the CC&Rs have much more success in the long run in preventing or controlling nonconforming changes.

Success for the association means success for all the owners too. A fight over architectural changes can become quite protracted, costly and vitriolic. It can change best friends and neighbors into worst enemies. A lawsuit can cost thousands of dollars, touching many—even those not directly involved—and often will completely polarize the parties. The players learn that there is no such thing as a friendly lawsuit.

On the flip side, inflexibility and resistance on the part of the board to consider even reasonable requests can cause unrest among the members. Almost everyone can understand why an association wouldn't want to approve a purple paint job. But in one case a homeowner wanted to paint her back door red—she had always wanted a red door. The door was located in such a position that *no one* but she and her guests could see it.

There were no specifically-stated color limitations in the CC&Rs and adoption of standards was left to the architectural committee. The owner was willing to keep the door in good condition and replace it with a conforming door or repaint it when she sold or moved out. Her association board said, "No way."

She painted the door red anyway. The battle began and raged for more than a year. Up to the point of the board's inflexibility Miss Red Door had been an involved, community-minded citizen. No longer. Could such a battle really have been worth it for anyone involved?

Many boards feel constricted in making exceptions or granting variances or approving overall changes. Attorneys warn that *consistency is critical* to preserving the association's ongoing ability to enforce the CC&Rs and rules—and it is. But flexibility and consistency may go hand-in-hand. In the *red-door* case the board could have accepted the request—if its criteria for architectural standards had been flexible enough.

Allowing for some individuality without disrupting the overall scheme or harmony of the development will sometimes quiet the castle-dwellers—residents who tend to take pride in their homes. Boards, attorneys and property managers sometimes forget that *harmony* comes in many flavors and political unrest or owner discontent can be a lot more disruptive than a rose trellis or basketball standard. A willingness to compromise on the part of homeowners is also critical to CID living. Homeowners sometimes forget, or maybe never realize in the first place, that the CID concept is about cooperative living. Intelligent compromise on *placement* of the rose trellis or basketball standard might bring satisfaction for everyone and improve the community.

KEY POINT

Allowing for some individuality
without disrupting the overall
scheme or harmony of the
development will sometimes
quiet the castle-dwellers.

Accommodation for Handicapped Residents

Modification requests to accommodate handicapped individuals deserve special consideration by the board. California *Civil Code* §1360 requires associations to allow reasonable modifications designed for access to and from the living unit for handicapped residents. The law allows associations to require the person seeking the improvement to pay the related costs—even for common area modifications—and to remove the modifications when they leave the development. *The Fair Housing Amendments Act of 1988* (FHAA) and other federal laws generally apply to prevent discrimination in housing and to encourage consideration for the disabled as developments are built. *The Americans with Disabilities Act* (ADA) forces some accommodation with respect to hiring of handicapped persons and access to public facilities which may apply in some larger city-like CIDs.

CONDOGURU

SPEAKS

Q: *My condo garage door hinges are shot. I asked the manager to replace them but he said that they are my respon-*

sibility. I thought the association was responsible for the garage door since it's part of the structure.

CONDOGURU: All right, here's the deal. Your garage door is an *exclusive use common area*, meaning that you are the only one who uses it so you get to maintain it.

If lightning struck your garage and blew the door off, the association would probably have to replace it because the association has responsibility for the garage structure.

If you wanted to replace your solid wood door with a segmented metal door (with architectural committee approval, of course) it would be at your own expense and then you (and any subsequent owner of your unit) would be obligated to pay for replacement when lightning struck again. The association would only have to replace it with the original-type wood door.

El Cid

Don't forget to check those CC&Rs. They may say the *association* replaces garage doors (so that the association has ultimate control over keeping them looking nice). The CC&Rs may say the *owner* is responsible for replacing his or her garage door—and the type required may even be specified. The CC&Rs may also say if the owner refuses, the association can replace it and charge the homeowner individually to cover the costs. But how often does lightning strike anyway?

Q: *My daughter and I put sun windows in all my rooms (I love the light!) but as soon as all those little protrusions appeared on my*

roof, I got a message from the president of my condo association on my machine saying, "We have to talk NOW!" What's up?
—Sunshine

CONDOGURU: The jig is up, lady, now come out with your hands up. You may love the light but you still need some enlightenment. What you have done in the name of "cheeriness" could well make you very unhappy—very. Here is what I think *el presidente* is going to tell you in the gentlest terms: **Take them out!**

Your dilemma is many-fold. First *fold*: You didn't bother to get approval for your windows and you made changes to the structure of the building. Some other *folds*: Did you have an architect draw plans and evaluate how a lot of holes in the roof will affect the roof structure? Will the next maintenance man up there land in your kitchen sink? Who did the work? Was it a licensed (and insured) contractor? Your unit doesn't have cathedral ceilings in all the rooms so you must have made some structural changes inside. Did you have a city building permit?

The architectural approval process is there to prevent just what you did. You may have seriously weakened the structure of not only your unit but those on either side of you, but we'll find out for certain in the next earthquake.

The architectural committee verifies that not only the appearance standards for the modification are met, but that it also meets structural standards. They are allowed, by law, to hire an architect to evaluate your plans, but I guess that is a moot point.

Then there is the question of maintenance. Who do you think should be responsible when the roof leaks? What about the reroofing program starting next year—your little modification is going to affect that.

This is a serious matter and you may have to pay for restoration of the building to its original state.

Is that enough light, Sunny?

El Cid : There are other concerns from the legal point of view. Imagine what happens when five others see the light and want skylights in every room? If the board says no, they may have a legal battle on their hands (using your dollars to institute or defend the lawsuit). You may get sued to take the skylights out and have to defend (with your dollars getting spent on both sides of the lawsuit). The possibilities are endless.

The point is that some of the potential problems could have been identified or worked out on the front side of this issue: fewer holes in the roof, assumption of responsibility for removal when the roof is replaced and adjusted maintenance responsibilities, etc. Thinking no one will notice will backfire more often than not.

Rules, Regs, CC&Rs Policies and Architectural No-nos

Once Octavia Ormandy found time to study association documents she realized that her alligator farm would have to be relocated.

CHAPTER 3

Rules and Reasons

**If I leave one car in guest parking, why can't I
keep a horse in my garage?**

You may have heard that your condo is your castle, but someone else is king. Boo Boo, Dockers and Tulip could certainly comment on that. There are times when rules seem unfair or burdensome—usually when we find ourselves in violation. Regardless, rules are necessary if we are to maintain the appearance and value of our shared property and ensure the peaceful enjoyment of life for all. Remember why you chose a home in a CID, or why you are considering one now. It may be a matter of affordability alone—but even if that is the case, would you invest your savings and mortgage your future in a development where neighbors leave derelict cars in their driveways and park trucks and RVs in their front yards? What about an owner who feels his bright red house provides the proper accent in a beige neighborhood? How would you like laundry lines stretched across front lawns, where pit bulls, Great Danes and rottweilers run free guarding the castles and marking their territories? Or your upstairs neighbor conducting aerobics classes at 6 AM? Without rules, anything is possible, especially disputes between neighbors. Everyone benefits from reasonable regulation—those already living in CIDs, new purchasers, and temporary tenants all have a right to expect a respectable quality of life and preservation of property values.

KEY POINT
Reasonable rules benefit everyone—present and future residents—and help prevent or clear up misunderstandings between neighbors.

Most everyone recognizes that purchasing a single-family home brings greater freedom coupled with greater responsibility than purchasing in a shared-wall environment. For those unwilling to accept the concept of cooperative living, buying a condominium or in any common interest development is probably a poor choice. The lifestyle needn't be unnecessarily inhibiting, but if your image of the American dream is tarnished by CC&Rs, then CID life won't be your style. Worse, if you are unhappy and take your displeasure beyond your walls then you can turn the dreams of your neighbors to nightmares. No homeowner can battle the association without in some way affecting every other member—his or her partners in cooperative living. When disputes are protracted or expensive, your neighbors are going to be hurt regardless of who wins—and so are you. Better that people become educated and make intelligent, informed choices *before* purchasing a CID home.

The reality for most residents is that rules are not a burden because they reflect the way a reasonable person acts—someone who is considerate of neighbors. In fact, many people choose common interest developments for their uniformity and rule enforcement power, so that they can be assured the look and feel of the neighborhood won't change drastically or adversely affect their property value. Obtaining rule compliance by the majority of residents requires little effort by the association beyond distributing the rule books and occasional reminders. Periodic notices, newsletter articles, and updates of established rules and policies give the homeowners an understanding of what is acceptable. In this society most people do what is expected of them, so setting some expectations isn't harmful—it's helpful. Reinforcement of civilities that are expected of all neighbors regarding parking, pets and conduct deters those who might otherwise ignore common courtesies.

Enforcement, however, can be a dirty word to some— namely the violators. Those who avoided reading the pile of papers stacked before them during escrow and who continuously set aside association mail for later are in for a surprise when they get their first notice of violation. Court battles over enforcement—or lack of it—the board's authority, the meaning of CC&Rs and rules, and the extent of individual rights litter the casebooks like flotsam along a beach. Homeowners can be sued by other owners or by the board for violating the CC&Rs or rules. Owners sue boards for not suing other owners to enforce the CC&Rs and rules. The sheer magnitude of cases dealing with common interest development disputes engendered a law that went into effect in 1994 encouraging alternative dispute resolution (ADR) before lawsuits are filed. (See Chapter 6 for more on ADR.)

Boo Boo, Dockers and Tulip (mentioned earlier) are three cats belonging to Natore Nahrstedt, a woman who fought her association to keep her cats in a no-pets condominium all the way to the California Supreme Court—and lost in 1994.

It doesn't have to be like this and in the majority of CIDs it isn't, but happy CID owners, unlike Natore Nahrstedt, are not newsworthy so you don't read much about them.

Rule enforcement is the responsibility of the volunteer CID board of directors, but the board cannot do it alone. It takes the involvement and cooperation of residents. At times, enforcement of a rule leads to a battle between an unreasonable homeowner (or tenant) and the board—or an unreasonable board (yes, they exist) and a homeowner.

There is little that other owners or the board can do to avoid the occasional rebel. Lured into an affordable CID by the enticement of home ownership, the rebel bristles at the thought of anyone telling him what to do in his own home.

Attracted to service on the board by the thought of greater status in the neighborhood, an otherwise amenable, affable homeowner can take a turn for the worse. Hunger for power is the worst reason to become a director because the power *must* be exercised with delicacy and reasonableness. Boards that are frustrated in getting residents to comply with rules, get along with their neighbors,

How Some People View CID Life

Of course I'm going to kiss you, Gwendolyn, just as soon as I check whether it's an approved common area activity.

pay overdue assessments, vote at elections, or take a volunteer position, can overreact and use power unwisely. The directors may be expected to please all the owners—an impossibility, Often the best they can hope for is to get understanding from those who can't be pleased.

Rules must be reasonable to be enforceable and understandable to get support from the membership—and support is required before compliance can be expected. As times change laws change. New cases are decided and some rules are no longer considered reasonable. Other events may invite new rules. Rules are a constant concern for boards and owners.

KEY POINT

A good rule is one the authorities
can enforce without looking
like a bunch of fools.
—Condoguru

The reason for a rule is not always obvious. Sometimes, people need to be told more. Savvy directors and property managers who want to avoid the prospect of dealing with angry residents, violation hearings and battles to collect fines, wisely keep residents informed as to *why* a rule exists. This can be done with articles in the association's newsletter, and a well-written, easy-to-read rule book. Too many CIDs circulate nothing, or distribute a rule book containing little else but a terse recitation of rules. Why not explain a rule's purpose in the rule book? Why not explain the concept behind the rules in general? Associations don't gain credibility by enforcing rules merely to punish individual conduct. Reasonable rules, intelligently written and understandable in their purpose, aren't usually the rules that become subjects of cat fights (apologies to Boo Boo, Dockers and Tulip). Rule enforcement should *correct*, rather than punish. Ideally, rules are reviewed annually to see if they conflict with any new laws, and to see if they are *working!*

People, Pets and Parking

Speaking of cats, we must remember that the law of the jungle does not apply in high density neighborhoods. To preserve civilization most of us agree that people must live by certain rules. Of course, accepting social regulation is easier in the abstract, or in the larger sense (government-type regulation). When we, ourselves, do something that we think should be perfectly legitimate, we could be inviting enforcement action. We might then view rules, and those *fools* enforcing them in a different light.

Enforcement—a negative-sounding word built around *force*. Who wants to be *forced*? What happened to freedom?

Ask any association property manager or board member for the **BIG THREE** enforcement issues and you'll hear: people, pets and parking—the *three P's*. Seminars for CID directors and managers typically carry titles such as: *Dealing with Difficult People* or *What Boo Boo, Dockers and Tulip Think of CIDs* or *One Man's Bronco—Another Man's Rolls Royce*.

The reason people often give for ignoring rules is that they infringe upon their freedom. We Americans are (rightly) concerned with our freedoms and loath to give up any of them. The *dirt* we live on is closely tied to our concept of individual liberty. We indignantly ask: Why can't I park my RV where I want? Why can't I swim with my dog after ten o'clock when no one else is using the pool? Why can't I have a booze bash in the clubhouse on Super Bowl Sunday? Why can't I hang my underwear over the balcony? This is America!

Reasonableness

"What we have here is a failure to communicate," said the warden, actor Strother Martin, in the film *Cool Hand Luke,* a moment before dispatching convict Paul Newman with a blow to the head. Perhaps he should have said that there was a failure to *obey* on the part of Luke. Communication was lacking, true enough. In a prison setting respectful communication is nice but not a necessity. Among the population of a CID, it is indispensable.

Understanding the reason for a rule makes it much easier for people to swallow and follow. A resident receiving a notice of violation is much less likely at the moment to be concerned with the reasoned debate among committee members who devised the rule than he is with the anger or embarrassment at being cited. When the notice is received, one feels much the same as when stopped by a cop for speeding—*Just write the ticket and let me get out of here before anyone I know sees me.* Once the initial adrenaline rush has subsided and the anger at the policeman dies down, one often admits they *were* breaking the law, accepts the medicine and goes on (perhaps somewhat slower for a time). It's highly unlikely that among reasonable people there will be much resistance if the rule is truly reasonable and serves a legitimate, understandable purpose.

A well-crafted rule: 1) is a deterrent to the prohibited conduct, 2) is easier to enforce than a patently unreasonable rule, 3) makes sense for the association to enforce, 4) is not likely to serve as the basis for a lawsuit, and 5) provides a helpful defense if a lawsuit does occur.

KEY POINT
Good rules are reasonable, enforceable, deter further violations, and have a lower likelihood of generating lawsuits.

Rule Review

Rules and enforcement are everyone's business. Association directors, resident owners, non-resident owners, non-owner residents, guests, tradespersons, managers and association advisers (legal, insurance, architectural, etc.)—are all touched in some way by the rules.

Periodic reviews of an association's rules by a cross-section of the community serving in committee is a wise policy. Obsolete or arbitrary rules should be deleted from rule books and rules needed to address changing times or new laws should be added. Without periodic review and feedback from owners, residents and association advisors, rule books become less and less relevant and the rules themselves less enforceable.

As each rule is considered, the committee might ask itself or others: Does this make sense? Is there a good reason to have it? Is there legal authority for the rule? Can the board enforce it without excessive cost or infringement upon people's lives? Does it help preserve the value of the property and assure residents the quiet enjoyment of their homes? If answers are negative then deletion or modification of the rule should be considered. A rule book will be more effective if it is written in simple, clear and understandable language and contains not only the rules but the reasons for them. It is generally counterproductive to have the association attorney write the rule book since simplicity is the key. However, a knowledgeable community association attorney ought to do a thorough review before the rules are distributed to prevent unintended consequences.

Some boards have been known to rewrite the rules without attention to the CC&Rs. Boards that do not know enough about current laws may not realize the serious implications in prohibiting day care facilities, solar installations, and in drafting age-restrictive rules. Restrictions must not be in conflict with laws such as the *Fair Housing Amendments Act of 1988*, the *Unruh Civil Rights Act* (California), and the *Americans with Disabilities Act*.

You mean they only fine you?
Our CC&Rs allow flogging.

One CID had a potentially serious problem with children riding bikes and skateboards on sidewalks. Sometimes rules that target a certain age group are risky because of laws that prohibit discrimination based on age, but this CID explained the restrictions in such a way that the homeowners understood the board's position and member liability and enforcement became much easier. Children even came to the CID president asking whether roller skates were allowed (they were) in lieu of skateboards. The association published a newsletter article that detailed the necessity for the restrictions and the importance of compliance, and conditions were soon improved. The article is reprinted here in an edited version.

Bicycles, Skateboards, Motorized Toys Prohibited on Walkways and Landscaping

"Let 'em have their fun. What are they hurting?"

How does one answer such a question without sounding like an ogre? Who would want to deny children the fun of riding skateboards, bicycles or motorized toys? This is a question that the association has to face even though some residents will believe such restrictions are too, well, restrictive.

Skateboards and bicycles are everywhere and everywhere you can see signs prohibiting them. Most often, increased liability is cited as the reason. Nirvana Homeowners Association is no different than the larger municipality in which we are located. The association faces possible lawsuit for injuries that occur in the common area.

Speed and Judgment

Bicycles especially, but skateboards too, can reach speeds that are unsafe for their riders and pose a threat to others. The sidewalks at Nirvana are too narrow to safely accommodate speeding skateboarders, bicyclists, motorized riding toys and the pedestrians for whom the sidewalks were designed. And while the young people on wheels have rapid reflexes and can perform enviable feats of balance, the missing element is the judgment that we have a right to expect from adults. These children come equipped with a sense of daring and immortality that we admire in our military fighter pilots and Navy Seals.

Peaceful Enjoyment

All residents, whether they own or rent their unit, are entitled to peaceful enjoyment of the property. That includes freedom to use the footpaths without fear of being forced to dodge bicycles or skateboards or motorized vehicles.

The distinctive sound of tiny wheels clacking over concrete expansion joints and the noise of repetitious maneuvers qualify (to most folks over thirty years old) as torture.

Safety and Liability

Few children seem to bother with recommended safety gear. Helmets, elbow and knee pads are common sense minimum protection. The State has mandated helmets for young bicyclists—a widely ignored law.

Skateboarding, even responsible skateboarding, can lead to serious injuries, even death, for the rider and at times, bystanders or pedestrians. Regardless of why the accident occurred, redress is often sought from the owner of the property where it happened, whether the owner had control over the elements or not.

CONDOGURU SPEAKS

People

Q: *I'm confused about what constitutes an acceptable window covering. My association's rules are pretty vague about this. For example, my teenage son likes black and silver walls in his bedroom and wants to paint the insides of the windows black. Is that okay?*

CONDOGURU: First, check to see if your teenager is okay. It is all a matter of taste, don't you know. Being the undisputed arbiter of culture the ol' Guru cleaves mightily to the one undeniable truth about taste. **There is no accounting for some peoples'.** I, of course, know instinctively what is tasteful and right. However, since most people lack my sensitivity I devised a method to referee questions of taste, specifically in dealing with window coverings.

I randomly selected three **U**nsuspecting **C**itizens of **M**oderate **I**ntelligence (no one would admit to average intelligence), hereinafter known as UCMI-1, -2 and -3. I escorted them to your home and asked for an evaluation of each window from the outside (since none were eager to step inside your son's room). I recorded their evaluations and play them back for you here.

WINDOW #1

UCMI-1: I'm not crazy about the aluminum foil lightning bolts.

UCMI-2: It does have a certain urgency but I agree that it clashes with the shrubbery.

UCMI-3: I sort'a get the urge to throw a rock.

WINDOW #2

UCMI-1: Well, they *are* drapes, and they are in good shape, but the woodland camouflage colors don't really go with the exterior paint.

UCMI-2: This certainly doesn't clash with the shrubbery... there is shrubbery here somewhere, isn't there?

UCMI-3: I used to wear something like that in Vietnam.

WINDOW #3

UCMI-1: Blue is nice. I like blue. Not that particular shade, but I like blue. Maybe if it were more on the teal side.

UCMI-2: Are you kidding? With the surrounding colors, blue sticks out like a musk ox in church. *On the teal side*—sheesh! I suppose you like *mauve* and *taupe*, too.

UCMI-1: It's doubtful that someone of your dubious heritage would know the difference.

UCMI-2: Oh, yeah! Well, with the way your nose is stuck up in the air it's a wonder you don't drown when it rains.

UCMI-1: Nobody talks that way to me, you worm!

UCMI-2: Oh, yeah! Want me to say it again? You're the worm. Worm, worm, worm!

UCMI-3: This one makes me want to throw a rock too. I ever tell you about 'nam?

At that point all three were arrested and now face charges for boorishness. Ol' Guru was not party to this disgusting display (being well hidden in the shrubbery—I think—near window #2). While failing to answer your question this revolting tableau does, however, illustrate the difficulty in devising rules or finding consensus on subjective items.

Your answer is simple enough—depending on who you talk to. Window coverings that draw attention probably don't blend with the decor of the building. Take a look and see what your neighbors see. By the way, black and silver walls can grow on you. I stayed in a hotel in Las Vegas with rooms just like that.

Q: *My kids were told they couldn't play in the tennis court. Why?*

CONDOGURU: I take it you're not a tennis player or you wouldn't ask. There are actually a couple of good reasons children aren't allowed to play on the tennis court. The big one is that the court surface is expensive to repair and can be damaged easily by skates, bicycles, skateboards and kids with braces who fall down face first. The other, and some folks insist, main reason is safety. A few ingenious tykes have managed to get the gates open without a key (something they could teach the association locksmith). Once inside, if they are injured, less clever adults might have a hard time getting to them. Besides, blood clashes with the color scheme.

El Cid

Of course, Guru, if the children are there to play *tennis*, we need to remember that rules excluding certain age groups from using the facilities are frowned upon, especially by El HUD.

Pets

Q: *Someone's French poodle has been using my front porch and the lawn near my condo for a restroom.*

CONDOGURU: Thanks for bringing up one of my favorite subjects. This falls in the *nuisance animal* category, but I think *nuisance animal owner* is more *apropos* (that's French for apropos).

The dog is only doing what nature equipped it to do. It is the owner's responsibility to maintain control of his or her animal (yes, cats too) at all times. Both city and county ordinances apply where you live and do not allow less restrictive association rules. Most associations require dogs be kept on a leash while outside for human safety and to prevent common area damage.

Plain old horse sense and courtesy should always prevail, but since not everyone has their full share, associations have rules that say owners are responsible for retrieving their animal's waste promptly and sealing it in plastic bags for disposal so flies and vermin aren't attracted. Yep, we actually have to tell people that.

Who hasn't experienced the joy of stepping in an animal souvenir? That is bad in itself, but we ought to think about the children who play on the lawns. They got no sense (other peoples' kids) and are susceptible to diseases spread by animal waste.

Animals that are a nuisance or dangerous could be turned over to animal control authorities for disposal. Seems like the irresponsible animal owner should be turned over for disposal instead.

The best thing you can do when you witness an owner failing to clean up after Fido (that's *Phydeaux* in French) is try to find out where he or she lives and report the incident to management. You don't have to collect the evidence. DNA matching for dog doo doo is not yet recognized by the courts.

El Cid: Good answer, Guru, but I've got a *however*. Some associations may get themselves into deep doo doo by removing unleashed pets (for disposal) *if there hasn't been notice to the animal owner*. That is sometimes hard to do when pets are free-roaming. The CC&Rs and rules should specify removal as a possibility and notice must be given **by some means** to residents that their precious pets could be captured for dirty deeds **before** removal occurs.

P.S. I'm checking my legal bag of tricks to see if there is any way to remove irresponsible animal owners. Some associations use fining—with proper authority and notice of course—to get the owner's attention. Some buy *pooper scoopers* and place them at strategic locations as a reminder—or perhaps to encourage a heightened social consciousness? So far, no authority exists to evict the owner along with the pet.

Parking

Q*: When can the management have a car towed legally?*

CONDOGURU: I think it is important to understand that management is an agent of the association, so it is within the discretionary powers given by the board that the manager orders a car to be towed.

Generally, a car is towed because 1) it is in a spot for more than a certain time; is inoperative; doesn't have a current registration; presents a hazard or nuisance; is dripping fluids; is not street legal, or prevents other cars from being parked; or 2) is not in a marked space or; 3) is unattended in a red zone. Number one usually occurs when a car is *stored* rather than *parked.* Number two could present a hazard to navigation. Number three presents a hindrance to emergency vehicles. Sometimes, depending on street configuration the area in front of closed garage doors is considered a red zone.

Q*: My car got towed away and I'm mad as hell about having to pay over a hundred dollars to get it back. What is it, you guys get a kickback?*

CONDOGURU: The great and noble Guru will excuse your intemperate remark about kickbacks. I'd love to get something out of this besides writer's cramp. Your car was towed because it was *illegally parked* in a fire lane—you know, the **RED** curbs.

California *Vehicle Code* provides for removal of vehicles parked in a fire zone or within 15 feet of a hydrant *without notice*. Towing isn't done arbitrarily, but by law. Before the tow truck driver hauls away any vehicle he takes a photograph to establish that that car was parked illegally. A representative of the association is on hand to supervise. The Condoguru understands your anger at getting caught and begs you, don't turn it inward. Yes, face your anger, but park where you're supposed to and you'll live happily ever after.

El Cid: To take it a step further, and as Guru says, there are specific laws in California that regulate towing of vehicles from CIDs. Without getting too detailed—the laws are technical and good legal counsel in drafting a parking/towing policy is advisable—the requirements to tow vehicles in a CID involve posting of specifically described signs at the entrances to the development, reasonable notice to owners of intent to tow, direct authority from association representatives to the tow truck operator at the site, taking pictures of the violation (in tows without notice), and follow-up with the local police department to report the location of the towed vehicle. However, as Guru says, vehicles blocking fire lanes may be towed without notice. (See California *Vehicle Code* §22658.2 and related sections.) Some streets are narrow enough to be considered fire lanes without the red curbs. It is state law, so playing dumb won't work. There are no points earned for stupidity under California law or association rules.

Q: *My son and daughter-in-law are going to be visiting us and they have a forty-foot Winnebago. Since we are in a smaller condo and there is enough parking nearby, we thought that we'd have them park the motor home there and run a power cord from the night light fixture on the sidewalk nearby so they don't have to run their generator. We don't want to bother the neighbors. Any problem with that?*

CONDOGURU: Save me. At your association the only authorized RV parking is for storage (not living) in the RV lot and it is for residents only (not relatives). So your plans for an impromptu campground in the common area are pretty much ruined, which is a blessing in itself. This also helps you avoid your other plan to use (notice I didn't say *steal*) night-lighting electricity paid for by the association. In this case, avoidance of two wrongs makes one (you) right. Sorry but your kids can't park their RV on the property.

Pool
(The Fourth P)

Q: *The manager ran my kids out of the pool. What gives him...*

CONDOGURU: ...the right? The manager's authority is delegated to him by the board of directors who are supposed to enforce rules.

First check your children's birth certificates to be sure that they are all over fourteen.

Now, check your kids for the reason they were ejected. Repeat after me and ask each child in a gentle, caring voice, "Were you throwing hard-edged objects in the pool, dear?"

"Were you trying to drown kids half your size, sweetie?"

"Did you tell the manager he was a no-good, boot-lickin' toady with a marked propensity toward procrastination and sloth, dude?"

"Did you think you were going to get away with it, dirt bag?"

Q: *The spa used to be a haven for us adults to sit and unwind after work. What ever possessed the board of directors to let little kids use the spa? The water is green.*

CONDOGURU: Your board of directors was possessed by the noblest of human motives: fear of the law. There is no rule against children using the spa for the same reason there is no rule against senior citizens using the spa. Such prohibitions are called age discrimination. There must be rules (by law) against any person under the age of 14 in the pool or spa unless accompanied and *alertly* supervised by an authorized (owner or tenant) adult user. So, as long as children are properly supervised, they are allowed in the spa. That still leaves wide open the question of who supervises the adults.

There is a hitch for the kiddies. The spa is not a wading pool or a play pool. It isn't a place for water polo. Traditionally, spas are for quiet relaxation. In past times, children being children, rules were adopted to give adults a break from noisy, boisterous behavior in the spa. Since the little darlin's have every right to be in the spa, the only way to provide a modicum of peace is to disallow this kind of behavior by *anyone*. Just as there are quiet, well-behaved children (I've been told), there are adults who, shall we say, ain't got no couth or upbringin'. So a rule against *any* loud or boisterous actions that is applied across the board is *reasonable*.

Who, you may be thinking, is going to enforce this reasonable rule? It would seem that a word to the offending party by the offended party should be enough. We are civilized here, are we not?

Oh yeah, about the green water, that was an experiment in large batch lemon-lime Jell-O. Actually, with increased use, the spa needs more attention to keep the water chemistry balanced. The chlorinemeister has been notified to check the spa more often. Chlorine will clear up the water (but your hair will turn green).

Fines

Q: *I've got a couple of fines against me which I think are bogus and I want to fight them. I'm worried that if I don't pay them that I could lose my property.*

CONDOGURU: This is an area where there is considerable confusion over what can be done to deprive you of property. It stems from the difference between an *assessment* and a *fine.*

Liens against your property can be levied for failure to pay either regular or special assessments and charges accruing from the nonpayment (such as interest and attorney fees). Assessments are your monthly dues and any other extraordinary expense that all the other association members have to pay.

Regular assessments are planned and reflect known expenses for operating costs and reserve funds. Special assessments generally come about from unforeseen or emergency obligations such as earthquake insurance deductibles.

Fines, on the other hand, generally aren't a basis for a lien on property. Most often fines are levied because there is reason to believe you broke a rule and spanking is not an option.

Even though your property probably cannot be liened for fines there are other ways to collect them. One way is for the association to take you to small claims court and get a judgment.

El Cid: There is a another possible way, O Great One, for associations to collect fines in the same manner as assessments (with rights to lien and foreclose for non-payment)—it is called a CC&R amendment. Believe it or not, most associations I hear from don't have much luck in small claims court—or so I am told—they don't let us legal beagles in there. Those associations that are also having trouble getting people to follow the rules ask explainers of law (like *moi*) for help. Although I'm not keen on liening for non-payment of fines, I recognize problems in enforcement. I believe that an amendment, approved by the percentage of owners that it takes to amend the CC&Rs, which allows for monetary penalties (fines) to be accounted for and collected just like assessments would be upheld if challenged by a delinquent owner.

CONDOGURU: Nag, nag, nag.

CHAPTER 4

Rights, Wrongs and Expectations

**I know my rights, I'm not wrong, and
I expect you to meet my expectations.**

Sandy had been meaning to bring it up for sometime now—
the thing about the parking space near her unit. It occurred to
Sandy that the board was meeting that very night so she
might as well go let them know about it so they can fix it.

When Sandy arrived at the meeting (a half-hour after it had
started) the board members greeted her and then went back to their
discussion about water bills. When they started talking about trash
pickup she spoke up.

"Excuse me but I need you to fix a parking space because
it's too narrow."

"I'm sorry, Sandy," said the president as the other directors
fell silent, "but the time for addressing the board is the half hour
before the business meeting starts. If you would like I'll stay after
the meeting so we can talk or you can call me at home if you don't
want to wait around, or you could submit your request in writing if
you wish."

"Can't you just listen for a minute?" she responded, feeling
a little angry about being put off.

The president looked at the other directors who nodded assent.

"Okay, Sandy, we will take a brief recess from business."

"There is a parking space outside my unit that is too narrow," Sandy said, "and it should be widened."

"Are you having trouble parking your car in it?"

"No, but when my boyfriend parks his RV there the side door bangs up against a tree and he can't get out unless he backs it into the street. We're afraid some fool is going to come driving along and hit the rear end of the RV. The space needs to be wider or the tree cut down."

The RV was parked in violation of the CC&Rs which prohibited RV parking in common area spaces. The president told Sandy that the matter would require further investigation and he would call her later in the week to discuss it in detail. She left, still feeling put off because she did not get a promise to widen the parking space.

What's Wrong With This Picture?

First off, Sandy's interruption of an in-progress board meeting—although it's something that often occurs—was improper. Next, she was apparently unaware that parking the RV in a common area space was a CC&R violation. And last, no one suggested to her that if in fact her boyfriend was parking an RV in a common area spot, that it had to be moved. The board allowed her to leave expecting the president to address her request.

Residents living in common interest developments, unless they attend board meetings regularly—an oddity in itself—or unless they are veterans of board service, may believe the directors should be there for them, when needed, to swing into action without hesitation. Board members are elected officials who bear some accountability to the owners who elected them and who want their attention. But they have a responsibility to the entire community that may supersede the desires of an individual.

If a local state assembly member or congressional representative is in a business meeting with other elected officials, constituents would be expected to refrain from interrupting. They may be heard at a scheduled private meeting or at open forums. At the corporate board meeting of General Motors, no one would expect a shareholder to interrupt. In each case there is an established protocol for addressing the officials. A homeowner association requiring similar protocols is not inhibiting individual rights or being unfair, so long as there is an established policy and reasonable opportunity to address the board.

In Sandy's case we'll ignore for a moment that the RV was parked in violation of the CC&Rs. Let's assume the parking space *was* painted too narrow for a car to park. Sandy's best course would have been to draw a simple diagram showing the location of the space, measurements, and the width of nearby spaces. A written summary of the situation would help too.

Instead of waiting for the board meeting to bring it up, she could have contacted the president or manager, according to association policy, several days (or weeks) before the meeting. Then the problem could be put on the agenda as an item for discussion, and any necessary investigation, such as measuring the width of the space and other spaces nearby, could be done by the time the board had to make a decision on the issue.

It is possible that this problem, like many others, could have been corrected by the manager during normal maintenance *without* board involvement at all.

In most cases, residents who make an effort to help the board gather information are more likely to get quick resolution.

Considering Sandy's case, with the newly discovered CC&R violation, it would have been better for the board to merely respond to Sandy that RVs were not allowed to park in the common area and that the parking spaces are intended for cars and small pickups. As it was handled, the president of the association was left to deal with the problem. Neither a letter nor a telephone call would have made Sandy very happy, especially knowing they could have told her during the meeting, rather than making her wait for an answer she wouldn't be pleased with.

Few homeowners ever see the board in action at a business meeting. Consider the difference between these two boards. **Board A** is disorganized, distracted by constant interruptions. It strays from the agenda to answer audience interruptions and allows unelected members to participate in the debate—people who may not have any knowledge of the subject. **Board B** has set aside 15 minutes before the business meeting for a homeowner forum. Time is split equally among those wishing to speak. The president opens the business meeting with an announcement that the audience may observe but not participate. Then the board sticks to the agenda.

A homeowner with a problem doesn't want to wait for an answer, but the board that reacts without investigation, understanding, or discussion is not doing its job. Board meetings are for board business. The agenda may include issues raised by homeowners. This approach allows them to be handled in an orderly and even-handed manner. Even small associations have business to conduct. If it were efficient, practical or realistic to allow homeowner associations to be administered by the general membership, then there would be little need for an elected board, but rule by the masses is no rule at all.

KEY POINT

Board meetings are for directors to make decisions. Homeowners may get their issue on the agenda by asking the president to include it and by providing information well in advance.

Boards, as well, need to show sensitivity to the resident's desire to speak, to have reasonable access and a forum. Associations with a published, reasonable process for hearing residents' concerns or complaints tend to experience less confrontation. A simple process and form for written complaints, submitted early enough, give the board an opportunity to investigate. Wise directors resist snap decisions, especially where there may be political or legal ramifications, without investigation or professional opinions. Directors may want to check with neighboring associations to see if they have experienced similar problems or have devised creative solutions.

CIDs and the Law

In recent years a number of well-publicized cases have cast homeowner associations in a less-than-favorable light. People who rely on newspapers as their only source of information get the impression that condo living means trouble—unless, of course, they are reading real estate ads that tout condominium living as trouble-free, carefree living, without responsibility. The paradox is that when a newspaper is used to *sell condominiums* they are heavenly. But when a condominium story is used to *sell newspapers*, the concept of this kind of living is criticized. Good news stories about well-run, problem-free associations don't sell newspapers—sensationalism does. The result is that negative impressions about boards and CC&Rs are accentuated in the public mind. There is no denying there are horror stories about condo living—a draconian board, an unreasonable neighbor, or a managing agent skimming from the till. These are the exceptions among the thousands of good associations that don't make the news.

Is the Board Really the Villain?

The many selfless volunteers who give time to run associations are often accused of usurping the rights of owners. Some board members are overzealous in exercising their power. More often the board members are just trying to do their jobs.

The famous cat case—or infamous cat case, depending on your viewpoint—*Natore Nahrstedt v. Lakeside Village Condominium Association, Inc.* (1994) is just such an instance. The press billed it as cat lover versus a villainous board. The truth is, the case involved a woman who kept three cats in her condo, knowing that it was a violation of the CC&Rs, and a board of directors charged with the obligation of enforcing those CC&Rs. At stake was nothing less than the integrity of the CID concept.

The *Nahrstedt* case exemplifies what can go wrong when a relatively simple dispute escalates to the level of statewide concern.

The association asked Ms. Nahrstedt to remove the cats. When she did not, the association first levied fines then attempted to file a lien on her condominium unit. Ms. Nahrstedt filed a lawsuit claiming illegal fines, harassment, breach of privacy rights, and claimed the association did not have the right to enforce the pet ban against her if she did not let the cats outside.

Two appeals court judges said Ms. Nahrstedt should be able to keep Boo Boo, Dockers and Tulip if they did not disturb the neighbors. The third one wrote a scathing dissent to the decision. He saw the issue as a "global enforcement" question affecting all CC&Rs provisions, not simply a matter of cat lovers versus others.

The Lakeside Village Board of Directors appealed to the California Supreme Court. People across the state supported the appeal, feeling that the lower court's decision would have a devastating effect on any association's ability to enforce CC&Rs. Many voluntary *amicus curiae* ("friend of the court") briefs were filed in support of the association's position. The appeal court decision had turned upside down the notion that CC&Rs are presumed to be legal and that frightened board members throughout California who were responsible for enforcing rules.

On September 2, 1994 in a six-to-one decision in *Nahrstedt v Lakeside Village,* the California Supreme Court confirmed that CC&Rs are to be presumed reasonable and enforceable. California's highest court helped to clarify the word *reasonable* which is liberally used by the state legislature when enacting laws and by the courts in analyzing people's actions. The court ruled in *Nahrstedt* that CC&Rs were to be *presumed* reasonable and *"...such restrictions should be enforced unless they are wholly arbitrary, violate a fundamental public policy, or impose a burden on the use of the affected land that far outweighs any benefit."*

What this means to the average person is that CC&Rs will be upheld unless they serve no purpose or are being applied in a manner that is fundamentally unfair.

The Supreme Court justices supporting the association's position intended that owners seeking *personal exemptions* from the restrictions should be discouraged. The decision promotes stability and predictability of CC&R enforcement in CIDs.

A condo purchaser or owner can count on the promises in the CC&Rs. Owners ignoring the CC&Rs do so at greater risk.

KEY POINT

The *Nahrstedt* decision gave CC&Rs a presumption of validity and placed the burden on the homeowner challenging them to prove that they are unreasonable or fundamentally unfair.

This decision will help boards of directors realistically evaluate their association's CC&Rs, rules and enforcement methods and decide what to do when there is a violation.

Is the Board a Friend?

The association is, collectively, all its members. The directors come from that pool of people. Boards are seldom diabolical or oppressive. They consist of owner-neighbors who have volunteered to help run things. Even though some run for the board to further personal interests or exert control, many recognize their duty to keep the good of the community in mind and to protect property values. *Community* is an attractive concept. Typically, directors care deeply about their community and are willing to accept the often unpopular task of making it operate efficiently and within the vast and confusing arena of condo law.

So how does trouble start to brew in condo associations? Disputes between the board and homeowners or neighboring residents happen because *life* happens. People want to be comfortable, happy, and have things their way—but in a CID buyers don't get to choose their neighbors and they often live in close proximity to each other, sharing walls and stairways.

When neighbors act neighborly disputes are rare, but disagreements inevitably arise in direct correlation to diminishing space. Some irritations become full-blown disputes. A 1994 law addresses this problem and helps associations and their members settle their differences before the courts become involved. The Alternative Dispute Resolution (ADR) amendment to *Civil Code* §1354 encourages parties to try mediation or arbitration before a lawsuit is filed. The law represents positive movement toward settlement of disputes and reduced litigation. Alternative dispute resolution is covered in detail in Chapter 6.

Good Neighbors

The quality of the condominium lifestyle depends in large part on the quality of the neighbors sharing a common wall or fence. In order to preserve tranquillity, an association must have the power to force compliance by those few who refuse to honor their commitment (made at time of purchase) to follow the CC&Rs. Whether a particular restriction is reasonable is subject to interpretation but it is far better to search for agreement within the local community than in front of a judge or jury. When the decision is left to someone else, no one really wins. The victory comes from success within the community. Many stand to lose when some disinterested party is given power to decide the dispute, for decisions which set precedent in court today may become de facto law tomorrow and legislation the day after.

The *Nahrstedt* case was intently watched by homeowner associations around California. Had Nahrstedt prevailed, the decision would question the ability of CIDs to enforce other reasonable rules. The case cut right to the heart of the entire concept of community associations.

What It Means

The *Nahrstedt* decision is a reaffirmation of the underlying principle of CID living. For the benefits derived from cooperative ownership, whether it be shared amenities, freedom from maintenance, harmonious aesthetics, extra security, or a concerted effort by others to preserve property values, CID members agree (as a condition of purchase) to abide by this *solemn written instrument,* as California Supreme Court Justice Kennard so aptly described CC&Rs. Had Ms. Nahrstedt been victorious, the very foundation of the association's ability to function would have buckled in deference to the self-interest of a single homeowner.

CONDOGURU
SPEAKS

Q: *My neighbor has a Monterey pine that is hanging over the fence between us and dropping needles all over my patio. I'm tired of it.*

CONDOGURU: I apologize for *needling* you but did you *needle* your neighbor about this?

That should be the first step. Ask him or her to work with you on a solution. Your back yards (in condos) are *exclusive use common areas* and you share the fence between them. In simple terms, you could slice off your neighbor's tree at the fence line, but then you'd have to look at the amputated limbs.

Think about whether you derived any benefit from the tree over the years. Did it give you some privacy, shade or add beauty to the area? Does it need to come out? Would you cooperate with your neighbor to take it out and split the cost since you found the tree not to be objectionable for years?

Do you really want, 1) the board of directors to become involved and dictate an answer, 2) an adversarial relationship with your neighbor, or 3) pine cones in your punchbowl?

Go on...work it out.

El Cid

You need to be especially careful if you decide to trim your neighbor's tree roots. While you may be able to chop off offending limbs, your right to cut the tree's roots is less than assured. Courts have held that in some cases where the roots are clearly on the opposite side of the fence from the tree, that to cut them may weaken or kill the tree. If that happens, the tree owner could win the case. It will depend on whether the roots are doing damage or not. Proceed with caution and perhaps the advice of a lawyer and a tree surgeon.

Q: *My unit is up for sale. I told the real estate agent that he could put a "for sale" sign on my garage door. The property manager told me that it had to be removed and later he took it down. What right does he have to take **my** sign off **my** garage door?*

CONDOGURU: There are two possible answers to your question. The manager hates you and is out to get you and make you unhappy. That's one. The wrong one, but <u>one</u> nonetheless.

The second answer is not so neat but is probably the real reason the sign was taken down. You live in a condominium, so the buildings belong to all of the owners. You may have the obligation to replace your garage door when it needs it since it is an exclusive use item, but the association does normal outside maintenance such as painting. What this means is that all owners own your garage door. So it really isn't *your* garage door.

Since it isn't your garage door you can't authorize a real estate agent to put anything on it unless you first have approval from the association. If you check your association's rule book you'll probably find a section on signs under Architectural Rules. Generally, you can have a real estate sign under the following conditions: 1) you've received permission from the association, 2) you assume responsibility for any damage caused by mounting the sign, and 3) you notify the real estate company representing your property about these conditions. The law prevents the association from denying you a reasonable real estate sale sign.

A less-than-caring real estate agent might tell you that you don't have to get permission from the association or might just go ahead and post the sign. To the extent he or she posts signs on common area property without association approval, the agent could be reported to the California Real Estate Board. In any event, it is better to work with the association so there is no altercation over signs. If any potential buyers drive by and see the manager and you in fisticuffs, they'll hightail it into the sunset.

I can hear it now. "Boy am I glad I'm moving out of this chicken-(blank) place. Make a federal case out of a real estate sign!"

At the risk of sounding patronizing, it isn't just the sign. Your sign represents a small symptom of a much larger concern. One of the reasons that CID living is so attractive to many people is that CIDs are *attractive*. They are kept that way with some fairly restrictive rules that are meant to prevent your neighbors from making your life unpleasant by: 1) raising chickens in the backyard and selling the eggs on the sidewalk; 2) inviting a hundred and fifty friends to use the community swimming pool; 3) building a dog run on the front lawn (for the puppies evicted from the garage); or 4) parking a junk car in the lot.

Before the *Civil Code* change, an association could prevent owners from displaying an outside sign. Now the restrictions are merely to keep control on what signs are posted and where. And believe it or not, these restrictions are designed *for the sole purpose of keeping property values up and the units salable*. Now, there's some irony for you.

Q: *My neighbor is a nut. He plays his stereo late and loud and forever and he has no taste in music. I'm not even sure what he's playing. He's got the bass up so loud that all I get is thumping and the sound of my own dishes rattling.*

CONDOGURU: What a coincidence, he sounds like my downstairs neighbor. Used to bother me until my hearing went south. Played Tony Orlando and Dawn until dawn. "Knock three times on the ceiling if you want me..."

He did. I hid.

All right, you've got a problem with your neighbor. The first thing to do is make a truthful assessment of the severity of the problem without making claims that aren't backed up by the evidence. Is the stereo on *all the time* or some of the time? Is it actually rattling your dishes or were you just trying to get my attention with a little hyperbole? (Hy'•per•bo•le: exaggeration, as in: "You must cease engaging in hyperbole. I've told you a *million* times not to exaggerate!")

First: assess the true nature of the problem.

Second: speak calmly and rationally to your stupid fool of a neighbor. Tactfully explain the problem and gently ask if he will turn the thing down a few hundred decibels because he's drowning out the Blue Angels air show.

Third: assess your neighbor's response. Most people will make an attempt to live in peace since it's pretty hard to totally ignore someone if you happen to share a wall. And there is always a possibility of retaliation.

Fourth: if the problem persists, take the careful records that you have gathered to this point (You have been keeping careful records, haven't you?) and file a _written_ complaint with your association's management or board of directors.

You need to be aware that the board of directors will probably resist getting into a personality conflict between two neighbors over a minor problem. If your complaint doesn't comply with the procedures set up by your association (written, giving details, etc.), the directors will most likely ask you to do so before they will even consider becoming involved.

They aren't being obstinate or uncaring. They are simply aware of the pitfalls and personal liability that *they* face if due process is not observed. You see, even your neighbor has a right to be dealt with fairly (whether he deserves it or not).

If the board finds merit in your complaint following investigation, then a notice of violation will be sent giving the accused an opportunity to correct the problem. If that fails to persuade then a fine could be imposed. That requires the violator be given an opportunity to appear before the board to argue his case.

I realize that this seems like a complicated way to do things when you could just sock him in the mouth (and face arrest for assault and battery), but the board of directors has to follow the California *Civil Code* in these cases. Frankly, they'd rather *you* got arrested than them.

You may not appreciate the complaint procedure and all the safeguards yet, but you will. I happen to know that your neighbor on the other side sent in a detailed written complaint that *your* rattling dishes are keeping her awake.

El Cid: Don't forget to check Chapter 6 for the scoop on alternative dispute resolution. Disputes between neighbors don't always warrant board intervention. Many locales have a community-based conflict resolution service for just those sorts of battles. These groups may provide trained mediators to deal with neighborhood disputes. If there is no blatant CC&R or rule violation occurring and its more a matter of two neighbors just not liking each other, sometimes it is best for the board to stay out of it.

Q: *The board of directors at my association keeps moving the meeting date and place for association meetings. I get the feeling they are hiding out.*

CONDOGURU: Same thing happened to me with my wives. Wasn't until I got to the courthouse that I saw 'em, all of them. And you think you've got problems.

The Davis-Stirling Act (§1363(g)) says any member of the association (you) may attend meetings of the board of directors (them) except when they adjourn to an executive session to discuss sensitive matters relating to personnel, contracts, litigation, member discipline, and your odd clothing and bad haircut.

Check your CC&Rs and association bylaws for meeting notice requirements. You may find that it states a specific time and place such as, 7 PM on the third Wednesday each month at the association clubhouse. Or it may say at a time and place the board chooses and give a period of notification. In any case, you have a right to attend meetings and you can do that only if you know where they are going to be. The meeting notice may already be in your association newsletter. When the meetings are mobile, as you say your board's are, ask a director or the property manager where and when the meeting notice will be posted, then get a better hair-cut and lose the bellbottoms.

El Cid: In the event your board continues to be elusive, show them *this* passage: *Homeowners have a legal right to know when and where the board meetings are. Intentional actions by board members to exclude association members by lack of notice or to hold secret board meetings may subject them to legal action or worse—onerous notice laws enacted by legislators who just don't like that kind of thing.*

***Cooperative living requires a certain
amount of cooperation from everyone.***

CHAPTER 5

What To Do When You Don't Like It

Of course you can fight city hall. You *are* city hall.

Item: Board president places reserve funds with his personal stockbroker who invests them in long-term, high-risk instruments. Two percent of the association's money is lost when Orange County, California goes bankrupt. After the recall election, the association pays many thousands in penalties to get its money back. This all occurs while the association is in litigation over construction defects and needs reserves to pay its attorneys.

Item: Owners paint swastikas on their home to protest heavy-handed board enforcement over minor infractions. Sixty-five percent of the owners demand recall of the board for, among other things, instituting a roving tow truck patrol. The board president called the association's difficulties self-inflicted and identified the main problem as not keeping the people informed.

Item: Members of a community association formed the People for Unity group to protest board actions and to force a recall election. The board refused to count the votes, locked the ballots and proxies in a box, and turned it over to the county superior court. A "special master" counted the votes. The old board lost 690-13.

Item: A board of directors meets January 12 and rescinds the association ban against pets. Another, newly-elected board meets eighteen days later, declares the previous board's action invalid and reinstates the pet ban. A director on the earlier board bought a cat (during the intervening period) which she was ordered to remove.

Item: After four years of wrangling over eucalyptus trees that some owners liked, but which blocked the ocean views of others, the board of directors held a secret meeting and hired a contractor (without notice to homeowners) to remove 200 of the trees, hoping (apparently) no one would notice. Workers contracted to remove the trees were threatened with a shotgun and shoved around by angry homeowners. The sheriff responded. The board could face charges of breaking state law since the eucalyptus were infested with longhorned beetle borers and the trees cannot be transported at certain times of the year.

The worst thing about complaining to the board of directors is that they may appoint you to be chairman of a committee to fix what you're complaining about. So you have a choice—shut up or get busy. That's democracy to some and blatant coercion to others. The truth is, there are several feasible ways to take up an issue with the board. You can:

- **approach the board** with your concern but keep in mind you can't get them to do something that they don't have the power to do. Even if they don't like your idea right off, being a squeaky wheel works—sometimes.
- **work with the board**. Offer to head up a committee or provide some special expertise you possess to make recommendations for improvements or other community projects.
- **serve on the board**. Board positions are elected but sometimes vacancies can be filled by appointment. If you are visible you

save the directors the bother of having to find someone to appoint and you could be chosen without having to run for election if a vacancy opens up. If you want to be elected it often helps to campaign, to show the other residents what you want the board to do and how you would work toward that end. Collecting proxies before an election is known to work magic on a candidate's chance of being voted in.

- **rally homeowner support**. Short of running for election, you can garner support for your effort. If there is enough pressure the board will be forced to reexamine its position. At the very least your neighbors will become aware of what's going on. In California, if five percent of the owners are willing to sign a petition calling for a special meeting, the board is bound to call one, or the owners can hold their own meeting.

- **try to recall the board** if you don't like what they are doing. Recalls aren't easy but they can be done. In some cases, a recall attempt will serve as a wake-up alarm, stirring the board (and often the owners as well) into action. A recall means, of course, that candidates will have to be found to replace the recalled directors. This isn't always easy.

- **sue the board**. Remember, though, if you sue there are some secondary issues. You will probably have to try mediation or arbitration first. The directors can use association funds to defend themselves, so in a sense, as an association member, you may be suing yourself, so you better have a good reason.

- **move to the hills**. You may think this option is offered humorously, but it is *no joke*. If rules, regulations, their enforcement and the board's power to levy assessments and impact your financial affairs bother you, CID living may not be good for you—or you for it.

KEY POINT
The board will probably defend
your suit using association funds,
including assessments you have
paid. Before filing suit, it is best to
explore other options.

The important thing to remember is that what you want to do must be reasonable or the rest of the owners will think you are a nut. If you can't rally a bunch of neighbors to your cause, it may be an indicator that you should heed. If the people are behind you, you'll have more clout with the board. If you get your back up for the "principle of the thing" back off and take one more look.

Most directors have principles too. Those who don't will spare no expense proving it—at your expense. It helps to be sure you're right and reasonable before undertaking such a major challenge. Run the issue by other owners or even friends (assuming you can find some who can be objective). If your dispute is with a neighbor, call a local dispute resolution group first to check your options. If the dispute is with the board, you might want to call the same people or a CID attorney with experience in dispute resolution—a professional in association problems will best be able to advise you about your rights when challenging the board.

Tips For Success

Present your case in writing. This is crucial. Make enough copies for board members and the manager. Send it in well before the board meets so you can get on the agenda and the directors will have time to review your letter and do additional research. Sometimes the board will be able to devise an alternate solution if given the time and support. The manager may have the authority to fix the problem without board involvement.

**Homeowners should not expect the board of
directors to instantly solve their problems
simply because they crank up the volume.**

KEY POINT

Present your case in writing. Help the directors find a reason to do what you want. No one likes to be attacked at an open meeting—it makes people naturally defensive.

Directors are supposed to make reasonable business decisions. This is difficult while under attack. The angry homeowner who makes demands or criticizes without providing the board with relevant information or the opportunity to study the problem often polarizes board members in opposition to his interests. Boards are made up of volunteers who aren't paid for their service, and they deserve respect, as do the owners themselves.

Analyze the Authority

The board has levels of authority, within limits, commensurate with what is needed to carry on association business. A board, for example, may enter into contracts but often is limited to a term of one year's duration by the bylaws.

The association's directors can generally adopt or change a rule as long as it is in accordance with the CC&Rs or superseding law. Sometimes homeowner approval of rules is required by the CC&Rs. There may be circumstances where a board would be justified in adopting a rule that conflicts with the CC&Rs. This may happen when a law is passed that supersedes the CC&Rs. Statutes that specifically permit home day care facilities in CIDs or prevent age restrictions are two examples. There might be a rule adopted to allow security alarm system window stickers that violate the CC&Rs but are important to resident safety. The board should get good legal advice in these situations because the integrity of the CC&Rs may be at stake.

KEY POINT

Rules that do not agree with the CC&Rs
or superseding law may be unenforceable, so legal advice is helpful in
these situations.

While rules generally can be changed by the board, a
change to the CC&Rs takes approval of the owners and in some
cases the first mortgage lenders on the property. Sometimes
amendments require approval of governmental agencies. Often,
changes to the CC&Rs will take a supermajority affirmative vote,
such as two-thirds or three-fourths of the members, and this can
make changing CC&Rs a difficult task.

The directors usually have a certain amount of discretion
that allows them to set building and landscaping standards and approve architectural changes or modify common area landscaping.
Major changes or controversial alterations of the established standards, while they may be within the authority of the board, might
warrant investigation into the prevailing membership desires. Instead of balloting, a poll or survey of the membership could be
taken to achieve understanding of the community's consensus.

Operating within their scope of authority, the directors can
effect some changes on their own. For issues beyond their powers,
they can put the machinery into motion that results in a change that
may or may not reflect the community's wishes. The board can
launch the legal work and mail-in balloting for a CC&R update,
long-term contracts, or significant changes to the common area. A
well-worded ballot often brings success. The greatest enemy to a
balloting campaign for change, though, is more often apathy than
opposition, but organized opposition can just as easily kill a ballot
measure.

Getting the board to act, to use its powers and authority
with care, or to change things takes *effort*. That effort might be

more positively and effectively expended cooperating with the board rather than fighting it.

Recall—Is It Really a Solution?

Recall efforts often run aground because their leaders don't maintain the drive and persistence necessary to rally support of the neighbors. Maybe they don't even involve the neighbors. Recall may not be the best approach even though it is often the first thing that comes to mind. On the other hand, it may be the only viable alternative in a situation where the board refuses to listen or where the support is overwhelmingly against the board.

Regardless of the outcome that is sought there are some practical considerations that should be addressed in any decision to challenge the board. What is the cost in dollars? in energy? in time? in frustration? What is the chance of success and the political cost?

Actions that result in litigation are expensive. It is not un-common for a homeowner who has been ordered to remove an un-authorized architectural change to fight the association in court and lose. The homeowner may well have to remove the change and end up paying his own legal expenses *and* the association's as well.

When the board of directors loses in court, trust, harmony and often the integrity of the association's regulating documents is diluted or lost altogether. Is it worth the cost? It may be, but that is something that all parties at risk for paying the tab ought to con-sider. This points up the necessity of taking a reasonable position and seeking resolution in other ways. When a board is challenged, it must defend. That same board, offered a reasoned argument at the outset for making a rule change or an exception for an architec-tural change, may well try to accommodate the request.

***When unit 5B owners wanted their section reroofed, the
Valhalla reroofing committee met to evaluate the
task before them. They quickly adjourned to a
local tavern and have refused to come out.***

Rational discussions, mediation and arbitration are generally lower cost, emotion-preserving methods that should all be ex-
plored before filing a lawsuit. The legal and political methods are
options that can work if they are applied in a rational way. It is,
however, disrupting to community life when members of an association, built on the concept of cooperative living, are forced to
choose sides. Friendships are challenged, neighbors divided, directors may be polarized, and wounds inflicted in the fabric of the
community may never fully heal.

CONDOGURU
SPEAKS

Q: *I want to be a board member but I don't know how to get elected. How do I get names and addresses of the people in my association so I can send them campaign literature?*

CONDOGURU: Before you start campaigning, check out the status of the board. In many cases, if there is a vacant seat, the directors can appoint a replacement. Show an interest, respiration and a pulse, and you may not have to campaign at all.

If there aren't any open positions, present yourself to the board as a nominee. If the nominating committee accepts your offer then the association may give you some exposure to the other members through the newsletter or in other mailings.

The situation at each CID is different. Sometimes the board has trouble finding enough candidates to fill the positions available. Others have hotly contested elections with scores of candidates going after a few seats. You need to test the waters and find out where your association fits in. A campaign may be unnecessary, but if it is, the names and addresses of association members can be supplied to you for that purpose. That's the interesting thing about apathy, by comparison the critically ill may seem highly active.

El Cid

If you want to send out campaign literature in California
CIDs you have some legal rights. You are also entitled to your very
own mailing list for this purpose under *Corporations Code* §8330.
Just ask in writing and be prepared to pay a small fee for the cost
of copies if your association is inclined to charge. If your association won't provide you with a list of members you may ask to have
your solicitation materials included in association mailings and pay
the extra mailing costs under provision of *Corporations Code*
§7524. Of course, if your association is strict on nominees and you
have difficulty getting nominated to run, consult an attorney. You
may be able to get elected by collecting proxies for a write-in candidacy or arranging a nomination from the floor if allowed in the
bylaws. You may get on the ballot by presenting a petition under
Corporations Code §7521. If this is what it takes to get nominated,
it is best to enlist the help of an attorney to explain the laws and
procedures.

Q: *I want to put a fountain in my back yard but the association has
a rule about "water-consuming" devices not being allowed. How
do I get around this?*

CONDOGURU: I'm shocked that you are asking me, the paragon
of virtue, to explain how to get around a rule? Okay, here goes.
Actually, you may not have to get around it. I think a frontal assault using the forces of logic might achieve your goal.

First, do your research. What is meant by "water-
consuming device?" That could mean hummingbird feeders or

lawn sprinklers—anything or nothing—could even mean people. I would suspect that water waste is a real problem for your association (as is writing a clear rule). If that's the case, find a fountain that recycles the water and needs minimum replenishment. Don't buy the fountain until after you get approval.

Now present your case in a clearly-written letter or on the form that your association provides. Show that you understand the need to conserve water, explain how your proposed fountain recycles water and needs only a few gallons a day for replenishment, try to get a copy of the manufacturer's specifications from the fountain store. I would say something like, it takes less than the equivalent of one flush of a toilet to maintain the water level and that you promise to not flush once each day to make up for it (levity probably won't hurt). Drainage is not a problem with so little water use. What reasonable board could turn down a request like that? Now all you need is a reasonable board.

Q: *I have been a director of my association for about three years and I need to step down from the board. My husband is having some problems with his health and I am going to have to take on another job soon. There is no way that I can continue on the board in good conscience but I don't want to leave them in the lurch. Other directors have just quit, walked away without a backward glance, and I have felt resentment for them because they just abandoned the rest of us without as much as a "by your leave." I want to depart with some grace, dignity and style and leave the others feeling kindly toward me.*

CONDOGURU: Are you this long-winded at board meetings? Sorry, I know, I'm *sure* the one to talk about long-winded people.

Here is how to do it with style that even Miss Manners would applaud. Write a letter to the president explaining the reasons you have to leave the board, express your regrets and offer to do what your schedule will allow to help in the future (such as serving on committees). Set a departure date as far in the future as you can (several months would be nice), *then start tracking down a replacement.* Take on the task as a moral duty because it is. Too often volunteers feel justified leaving on a moment's notice because they aren't paid. What they don't seem to understand is that the people whom they leave holding the bag don't get paid either. It is a matter of honor to finish a term as you indicated you would when you took on the task and title. If it becomes impossible to continue, as it is in your case, then the honorable thing is to help the others deal with your departure. Then you will leave without regret or resentment with your head held high, marching into the sunset, a victor in the game of life, proud, content with yourself. What a woman!

Q: *I am curious about some past board decisions. I seem to remember some motions they passed but sort of forgot about later when it would have been inconvenient to remember. How can I get a peek at the records of the meetings from years past and the later ones too?*

CONDOGURU: The name is Bond, James Bond, guru for hire. Should you choose to accept this mission the secretary will disavow any knowledge....

Forgive me. As much as I'd like to sell my espionage services, alas, they won't be needed. As an association member, with a security clearance at the Superfluous Level, you have a right to see the records. You will probably be prevented from taking originals with you but you can get copies. California *Corporations Code* allows you to inspect the accounting books, records and meeting minutes on written demand at a reasonable time (normal working hours) for any purpose that is reasonably related to your interests as a member.

The exception would be minutes of confidential meetings or executive sessions to discuss personnel or other issues requiring privacy and matters of litigation. The regular meeting minutes should reflect, in general, what the executive session was about.

Inexperienced directors may tend to deal with problems using simplistic methods.

CHAPTER 6

Alternative Dispute Resolution

Why not take 'em to court?

In this litigious society, with people ready to go to court as a first step in settling problems, everyone pays the price. The judicial system is **not** an institution that encourages us to get along with one another. In litigation, a judge hands down a decision and, although there is a judgment of the issue at hand, the inevitable result is polarization of the parties. Courts pick winners and losers and losers get no satisfaction. In homeowner cases, since an ongoing relationship is at stake, there are other, better ways—outside the courthouse—for community associations and owners to resolve disputes.

In homeowner associations a good place to start the resolution process is with a visit or friendly telephone call to the person with whom the disagreement has arisen. The caller should ask, "Can we solve this problem between us?" or "Can we talk about this problem or disagreement?" Talk is a first step.

Persistent arguments take a lot of effort and time. If the people involved are willing, many matters can be settled with a handshake. But someone has to break the ice.

*"I shan't marry you, Gwendolyn, however, I
will consider binding arbitration."*

Some CIDs use an intermediary to start the thaw between
the warring sides. They may rely on an appointed liaison or ombudsman to initiate talks. A congenial person who is not tied to
demanding family or business obligations and who can adopt a
disinterested view can work in this unique position and find great
personal satisfaction in helping solve problems.

If neighbors or intermediaries aren't able to find resolution,
the association manager or board of directors are next in line. With
the board, the dispute may have to be handled according to set procedures with due process and public or private hearings. To be effective, directors need something to work with—that means
documentation. Complaints to the board should be in writing. The
directors will need details: names, dates, specific acts, witnesses.
Acting on oral complaints is dangerous for all parties. In those ex-

treme cases where a written complaint might put an owner in danger of retaliation, then legal advice, police intervention, or other protections may be warranted.

If manager or board intervention doesn't resolve a dispute between association members or between members and the board, mediation or arbitration should be considered as the next step in the process. These are called alternative dispute resolution (ADR) methods because they offer recognized alternatives to litigation.

If mediation or arbitration fails, then the only answer is court—but only if it's going to be worth the bother and expense and if the parties can remember what the dispute was about.

When it's all over, you're still neighbors

In one clear case of going too far to prove a point a resident refused to remove "burglar bars" worth $60 that he had mounted outside a window of his unit. After several years of hassling with his association's board the case landed in court where he lost. The court found he had clearly violated architectural rules and was forced to pay not only his own attorney, but the association's legal fees of $30,000 too. Then he had to take down the bars. Through mediation, he might have been convinced to switch to interior bars that would not create a flap over aesthetics, but which would fulfill his need for security.

How do such petty cases end up in court? Sometimes it is simple bullheadedness on the part of either or both parties. An unwavering assertion that, "My home is my castle and no one is going to tell me what to do!" can spark a firestorm. Sometimes it is a simple misunderstanding of CC&Rs, or a *damn-the-torpedoes* stand on principle. Whatever the motivation of the litigants, these cases can be devastatingly expensive, divisive to a community, and destructive to property values for all.

Who wants to buy into a community in litigation? The possibility of an adverse court decision triggering a substantial special assessment is a red flag to potential buyers and lenders.

KEY POINT

Cases over trivial matters brought to court as a matter of principle can be devastatingly expensive, divide the community and adversely affect property values.

The CID Alternative Dispute Resolution Law

The California legislature, at the strong urging of community association industry groups, logged a law in the books, effective January 1, 1994, that encourages ADR in common interest developments. Section 1354 of *The Davis-Stirling Act* was amended to relieve courts of a growing number of lawsuits filed by associations and members seeking rulings on CC&R provisions.

The new statute is designed to short-circuit these lawsuits. Although it is a half-step shy of *requiring* ADR, it does give strong incentive to the parties involved to engage the other side in some form of ADR *before* a lawsuit is filed.

It works like this: the party with the grievance must prepare a "request for resolution" describing the complaint and requesting alternative dispute resolution and then serve this *request* on the other party. The receiving party has 30 days to respond. If there is no response, the complainer may file the lawsuit but must certify an attempt was made to engage the other side in ADR.

If the ADR request is accepted, the two parties decide on one of several means of resolution. If arbitration is chosen, the parties would decide ahead of time whether the arbitration will be binding or nonbinding. If agreement can't be reached on binding arbitration, any arbitration proceeding would be nonbinding.

The law applies to cases brought by the association against a member, a member against the association, or between members of the same association when the dispute arises from the CC&Rs.

The cases covered by the ADR law address CC&R or rule violations—pet restrictions, unauthorized architectural changes, elections and voting, meetings and board rules or policies. ADR procedures apply to monetary claims under $5,000. The penalty for not complying is that the party bringing the lawsuit may be denied the right to recover fees and costs if they win the case. If a party refuses the ADR request and loses in court, the judge may consider the refusal to engage in ADR and may award more attorney fees than he or she otherwise would if the party had agreed to try ADR first. There are other potentially more devastating punishments for failing to seek resolution by alternative means. The judge could decide to dismiss the lawsuit.

The ADR law is well-intentioned—not perfect—but a step in the right direction. Skeptics argue that disputes over interpretation of the law may arise, or that ADR is just another layer in the process, lengthening the period of time and costs necessary to reach a final judgment. Some cases might be protracted by this provision, but one would be hard pressed to argue that litigation is preferable when a nonjudicial resolution in homeowner disputes is possible.

What is Mediation?

Mediation can be a quick and relatively inexpensive dispute settlement procedure. Unlike arbitration, the mediator does not render a decision but instead works with the parties to help them reach agreement between themselves. Mediation provides a creative forum that offers the parties equal roles in reaching a mutually-acceptable resolution. The decision is *agreed upon* rather than dictated by a separate authority.

In binding arbitration an *arbitrator* hands down a decision that is final and carries the same force as a court judgment. The arbitrator has no obligation to consider what is best for the parties when imposing a resolution, nor does he or she face limitations— like following the law. A mediator, on the other hand, has a mission to help the parties understand each other and the dispute, and to work toward resolution. Trained mediators generally uphold this goal and refrain from trying to impose their ideas for resolution on the parties.

[Authors' Note: In this text we refer to "trained" mediators. People who present themselves as mediators but who have not had mediation process training are not likely to conduct real mediation. They may be good Joes (or Josephines) who feel they have an ability to pressure parties into a settlement, but the idea of mediation is to let the antagonists resolve the conflict themselves with the mediator providing the right kind of help and guidance.]

Mediation is a good first step when outside help is needed to solve arguments. It does, however, help when each party wants resolution of the *problem* rather than victory at the other person's expense. When people come to the table seeking a solution, even if they do not believe it is possible, a good mediator can lead them to success. When a determination to resolve the dispute permeates the talks, success rates run 80-90 percent. Mediation doesn't work as well when the parties would rather let someone else fix things—that's arbitration and litigation.

An association's problems can undermine a community if not handled properly or quickly. Small problems may grow rapidly into large ones. The nonadversarial nature of mediation actually promotes further cooperation. In a successful mediation both sides can win and walk away from the table with dignity.

Mediators manage conflict. They get people talking openly by assisting in the negotiations, by allowing them to release anger and energy while keeping enough order, authority and presence to maintain focus on the dispute rather than personalities. A good visualization is a balloon full (to bursting) of hot air—something like an angry homeowner. A skilled mediator knows how to release

*"Your choice, Sam, mediation, arbitration
or a skull fracture."*

some of that hot air so the balloon doesn't explode. As pressure is
released, the balloon becomes more flexible, even manageable, like
the long skinny ones magicians and clowns use to create novelty
hats and poodles at the fair. Creatively managing the conflict is the
key to a solution.

Mediators ask questions and may make suggestions to help each side learn what the other's expectations are and the basis for them. Once the situation is seen from the other side's viewpoint people are often more willing to compromise.

Mediators can also help with a *reality check* of the situation. For the three to four hours it takes to resolve the average dispute the cost is minimal. Even in cases where mediation fails to completely resolve the problem, all sides can realistically assess where they stand and get a good idea of what might happen in court should the case continue that far. Sometimes the stark realization of the cost and hassle of litigation puts the dispute into perspective. The matter may no longer seem important enough to pursue in court.

Mediation is often successful in turning enemies into allies. Even where an alliance does not occur, ongoing community relationships are preserved when there is voluntary agreement. That's important because when it's over, the people involved are still neighbors.

Whatever is said or presented in mediation is confidential. Statements and prepared documents cannot be used later in court as evidence against either party, and the mediator cannot be called as a court witness. This confidentiality is an additional benefit. Resolution can be sought without having to reveal personal, financial or embarrassing information or give away the store.

How Does Arbitration Differ?

An arbitrator acts much like a judge who hears arguments from both sides then renders a decision. There is no stifling formality of a courtroom. The rules are far more relaxed.

Binding arbitration—where the parties agree ahead of time that the decision will be *final*—most closely resembles a courtroom decision. To some it is a relief because it resolves the issues once and for all with minimal chance for appeal. Others find it scary because an arbitrator doesn't have to follow case law and in binding arbitration appeal rights are even more limited than for court decisions. Because of these factors, some see arbitrators as more powerful than judges.

An alternative to binding arbitration is *nonbinding* arbitration, in which case, either or both sides may reject the arbitrator's decision and go on to court. This method usually provides an objective evaluation of the matter while still allowing flexibility over whether to accept or reject the decision. As in mediation, nonbinding arbitration can be a reality check. The critics of nonbinding arbitration complain that it is nothing more than another layer of cost and time on the way to court. Arbitration costs can be high, approaching those of litigation, if there is extensive discovery, witnesses who have to be compensated for their time, use of experts, and if the matter is complicated.

ADR in all its forms can offer attractive, effective and less expensive ways to avoid court. Which form is right for any given dispute depends on the situation, the parties' willingness to work toward a compromise, and the problem at hand.

This increasingly popular approach to settlement is often found in consumer contracts. Agreements for many different products and services have a mandatory arbitration clause. There is controversy in the legal world as to whether imposition of binding arbitration (such as in health provider, banking and employment contracts) is constitutional, since the arbitrators do not have to follow the law and appeal rights are so limited. But where the parties are willing and open minded, they can benefit from an agreement to use mediation or arbitration to resolve differences.

Before agreeing on the ADR method all parties should become aware of their obligations. Responsibility for fees must be clarified. The agreement may be for each to pay half, one party to underwrite the initial costs, or the arbitrator may be left to ultimately decide the fees issue. Since at least a portion of the fee is generally paid up-front, this issue usually needs to be discussed ahead of time unless one party or the other is willing to make the necessary fee deposits.

CONDOGURU

SPEAKS

Q: I started putting a portable spa in the backyard of my unit. Then I got a notice that I have to get architectural approval before I finish work on the little concrete slab to mount it on. Why do I have to get architectural approval for a portable spa? Nobody is going to be able to see it except me.

CONDOGURU: A portable spa? I guess you mean one of those above-ground types rather than one that will fit under an airline seat as carry-on luggage. Or do you mean one that you can take with you when you sell your unit?

There are a couple of issues involved here. First, since you live in a condominium, the back yard is common area even though it is designated for your personal and exclusive use. Any significant change to any common area needs architectural approval. In many cases this is just for the purposes of documentation so there is a record of who is responsible for maintenance. This is important when you sell your unit because the new buyer has to be made aware that responsibility for the change you made passes to the new owner. That full-scale replica of Stonehenge that used to hold your portable spa now belongs to him or her.

How do you plan to heat several hundred gallons of water? Are you adding gas-fired equipment? And where will you put it?

How do you plan to vent the heater if it is inside? Will you be creating a fire hazard or adding unreasonably to the noise your neighbors hear?

There is also the question of drainage. Back yards where you live are all connected to a common drain system. If your alteration blocks drainage or overburdens the system's design, you could find yourself responsible for causing backyard floods or backups in other units on the same drain line.

And here is a big one that has to do with water use. Since your water bill is paid using association dues and you don't get a water bill of your own, you may not appreciate the cost of water for your one-person spa. Your neighbors will all have to contribute to a higher water bill so you can fill your spa periodically. That hardly seems fair, does it?

This is not meant to suggest that the architectural committee will not approve your spa, but so far your chances are better with the lottery.

Your request might be more kindly received if, for example, you happened to buy a spa that recycles water. That would be a point in your favor. If your plans clearly show how the back yard drainage is preserved, that's another point.

You getting the point?

Depending on the structure you plan putting in to hold your portable spa, you may need a city building permit. It's up to you to show whether you need one or not and to obtain it if you do.

The architectural committee and the board of directors are charged with responsibility for maintaining the value of the common property, including your back yard, through enforcement of reasonable rules to protect the prevailing style by controlling changes.

They could justifiably decide against your spa for any of the reasons cited. That's why it is so important to get approval first—*before* you spend your money on something that someone else has the right and perhaps, even duty, to tell you to take out. You could even face a fine.

Of course if you want to invite me over for a dip and a bottle of Chivas Regal, I could put in a word for you.

El Cid

And to ice your waters even more, the 1994 California Supreme Court decision in *Nahrstedt v. Lakeside Village Condominium Association* upheld the validity of CC&Rs unless an owner could prove they were completely arbitrary (as applied to all folks) or that they served no identifiable purpose, and noted that the oft-forgotten third party to these cases—the other owners—should be able to rely on CC&Rs being upheld. You're in over your head, pal.

PART 2

THE MONEY ANGLE

CHAPTER 7   DUES AND DON'TS

CHAPTER 8   PAYING FOR THE UNEXPECTED

CHAPTER 9   INSURANCE

CHAPTER 7

Dues and Don'ts

**Why do the directors keep raising my dues? What did
they do with the money I gave them last year?**

The simple answer in most cases is that they spent the money
from last year on budgeted and necessary expenses and that
they have no choice but to raise dues to meet new expenses.
Costs of operating just keep going up. *The Davis-Stirling Act*
(§1366) specifies that *"...the association shall levy regular and
special assessments sufficient to perform its obligations under the
governing documents and this title."*

The obligations in the association's *governing documents*
can't be ignored. Insurance, utilities, administrative costs, management, maintenance, repair and replacement of equipment and
structures are often substantial expenses outside control of the association. And the government or the courts will, at times, create
unexpected obligations as was the case when the California earthquake recovery fund legislation passed in 1993 and condominium
associations were assessed up to a $60 surcharge for each unit that
was owner-occupied. The fund proved unworkable and was later
abolished by the state. CIDs that paid into it lost their money. Associations had little say in the matter. Legislators and judges have

indirectly imposed other expenses and costs through laws and case decisions that pressure CID boards to purchase workers compensation insurance (even when there are no employees), to buy fidelity bond insurance (in excessive amounts), to fund reserves, to raise limits of liability insurance (a trade-off for statutory protection of homeowners), and to hire professional management and consulting services to minimize liability and to help sort out myriad legal requirements imposed on associations.

What makes the *money angle* such a challenge for CIDs?

Human nature for one thing. Cooperative community living depends, in large measure, on effectively dealing with and channeling the natural desires possessed by humans. Directors of CIDs are association members *as well as neighbors and friends* to those whose dues they may have to raise, and from whom they must collect—sometimes very vigorously.

No one wants to keep raising dues but there is not always a choice. People tend to have high expectations as to how the association will be maintained and run, yet bristle at having to pay the costs. They want the board to manage without having to pay a management company, without regard for the amount of work, dedication, time and expertise that is needed to do it right. Friendships often get in the way of fiscal responsibility. Being a *good director* can also mean being perceived as the enemy. Homeowners don't generally appreciate budget pressures facing directors. Without understanding the directors' job it's easy to criticize. Most board members give their energy and time for free and receive complaints in return.

Boards can avoid criticism in the short run by applying all dues collected to the operating budget, shortchanging reserves. People immediately notice if the grass isn't mowed, the pool isn't cleaned, or the water is shut off. But reserves are a *savings* account, there is no bill to pay every month. The reserve obligation could easily be ignored and directors and neighbors could remain friends—until the roofs give out and the piggy bank is empty.

Some cast stones at the board without offering solutions or even trying to understand. In *The Davis-Stirling Common Interest Development Act* directors, like the California condor, are recognized as an endangered species and are provided certain immunities under §1365.7. The legislators realized that they could not, on one hand, require that directors be volunteers with serious obligations to the community without, on the other, giving them relief from worry about liability arising from their service. Very few would volunteer if they faced personal financial risk for their decisions.

Of course, there is a flip side to the good guy directors—the bad guy directors. In one association, the president paid himself for airplane tickets (about $750) to fly back for a homeowners' meeting (to discuss his recall) from his father's sickbed in another state. The recall meeting was called because the board had lost control of the checkbook and there were other questionable payments to the (now) ex-president.

So, what rights to homeowners have? Notice, for one...

An owner is entitled to certain information about how the dues are spent. Between 45 and 60 days before each new association fiscal year begins the directors are required to send a *pro forma* budget to all owners (§1365).

Pro forma simply means a description provided ahead of time. There are various parts to this mailing: the annual operating budget, reserve allocations, assessment collection procedures, and an explanation of what special assessments might be required for the coming year. The tight timing, with its 15-day mailing window, is a real test for boards—especially those that are inefficient or disorganized. If they miss the deadline they are prevented by law from raising the dues for the next fiscal year without member approval.

This is a tough provision of the *Civil Code* (§1366). There are conceivable justifiable reasons for delay—not all of them the board's fault. If the deadline is not met and the dues are not increased when they need to be to pay bills, the insufficient income affects all owners and their properties. But this law is better than what was first proposed by one legislator—that if the deadline was missed, *no assessments* could be charged for the coming year.

It's certainly not fair or right to keep budget and financial information from the owners. It must be shared so that people who want to know how their money is being spent can find out.

KEY POINT
As a homeowner in a CID you have the right to know how your money is being spent. The annual pro forma budget should reflect anticipated operating and reserve needs and expected special assessments.

Annual Financial Review

Within 120 days after each fiscal year ends, an accountant's review of the association's finances must be given to all members if the association collected more than $75,000 in income (§1365). Additionally, owners have the right, subject to prescribed procedures, to view association financial books and records throughout the year. Some associations offer even more timely information and post a monthly "budget-to-actual" report or provide the financial information in a newsletter distributed to the owners. When more information is distributed, fewer questions arise. Openness about finances encourages trust. Secrecy breeds distrust. Sometimes a board decision not to share information is based on logistics, shortage of time or resources, or the perception that no one cares or pays attention anyway. Such a position, right or wrong, even when innocently motivated, can lead to claims of board secrecy.

"I think the board is being a little too secretive and free with our money."

"What makes you say that, surely not the limos parked outside their meetings?"

"Do you wish to imply that because no one has ever seen them in the daylight that something is afoul?"

"Could it be that this year the annual meeting is in Hong Kong?"

Reserves

The differences between reserves and operating funds is recognized by state law and the two funds are not supposed to be commingled. The *operating* budget covers day-to-day expenses. The *reserve* fund is for defined items that are prudent to save for—items such as reroofing, resurfacing the swimming pool or tennis court, replacing clubhouse furniture or perimeter fencing. The lawmakers in California periodically add restrictions designed to protect reserve accounts since they have been approached with homeowner stories of reserves having been raided. The laws are strict concerning annual disclosure of the reserve account standing. It has, in the past, been very tempting to meet operating fund short-falls by "reallocating" the reserves. This can eventually lead to se-rious economic problems, possibly even bankruptcy.

At the opposite extreme some boards have collected higher dues than were necessary, building large, undesignated cash sur-pluses rather than a defined contingency reserve. While such a move might appear responsible, it can also be a case of poor fiscal management. High monthly dues have a negative impact on poten-tial buyers. Unnecessarily hefty special assessments foment politi-cal battles—just as unnecessarily high taxes do.

What is Adequate?

The pro forma budget must contain specific information about the status of reserve accounts, the reserve study, the "percent funded" and whether any special assessments are anticipated in the coming year.

This "percent funded" figure is rarely 100 percent. So how is it possible that reserves totaling less than 100 percent of the identified need can be considered adequate? Should the board be striving for 100 percent cash in the bank, or is there some lesser amount that is acceptable?

Reserves are typically figured on what the association is *projected* to need over the next thirty years to repair, maintain or replace major improvements. Normal cash flow should make adequate funds available when needed if reserve contributions are set at the correct level. *Civil Code* §1366.1 requires the board to assess for the needs of the association. It does not encourage stockpiling huge amounts of money for which no purpose can be identified. In other words, an association is not expected to collect in 1995, all the funds that are going to be needed in the year 2000 for roofs. A portion of those funds should be collected in the intervening years so the necessary money will be available when needed. *Civil Code* §1365 requires that a reserve study be done every three years with annual reviews to make adjustments when warranted.

KEY POINT

Reserves that are funded at an adequate level will provide the *right amount of money at the right time* for planned future expenses.

In most cases the largest single reserve item that a CID needs to consider is roof replacement so, for the sake of simplicity and illustration, let's look at the roofing component of the reserves as an example, as calculated by one school of thought.

Reroofing in the Future

Heavenly Homeowner Association replaced all its roofs in 1990 for $500,000 using all the funds that were available, taking the roof reserve back to zero. The shingle roofs that were installed have a thirty-five year warranty and the underlying structure is in good shape. Since a lot can happen to a roof in thirty-five years, the board of directors decided to assume replacement would be required in thirty years (2020) with the same type of roof.

A reserve study projected the increased costs over the next thirty years. The directors set the reserve estimate at $1,000,000—twice the cost of the previous reroofing. This means that, $33,333 a year will have to be collected for roofing reserves. The directors divided the annual reserve requirement by twelve then by the number of units to set the amount each owner would have to pay (as part of monthly dues) to properly fund the roof reserves.

What about interest on the funds that are collected? Often, in a reserve study an assumption is made that interest (on conservative, safe investments) and inflation cancel each other out. This makes the numbers easier to deal with. And why shouldn't the process be easy as possible? There are so many variables in determining what funds will be needed in thirty years that it would be irresponsible to expect an exact science—a reasonable prediction based on available information must do.

Do Something

The point is that *some consideration* must be given to future needs and *some plan* must be put in place to avoid huge financial shortfalls. Since the reserve requirements have to be studied every three years, there will be at least nine studies done before the roofs need replacement at Heavenly HOA. Each study and annual review looks at the adequacy of the plan and refines the requirements year by year.

Returning to the original point, the roof reserves in 1991 were funded at about 3 percent of the full projected need, but in 2005 (midpoint in the existing roof's life) 50 percent of the required funds will have accumulated. ***In 2005, 50 percent funding is adequate and on target.***

Note that there are several ways "percent funding" can be expressed. An accumulation of *50 percent* of the roof reserves in 2005 could be legitimately identified as *100 percent funding* since the roof reserve accumulation is on target at that time. Check the method used for your reserve study.

Each reserve component item must be considered for its remaining life and expected cost to replace. Taken in total, the directors can set an amount to be saved each month and determine the reserve funding percentage against the total requirement.

The *operating budget* is based on one-year projections and can, therefore, be more accurate. Reserve funds can be borrowed to meet unforeseen operating shortfalls, emergencies, or for litigation related to the components, but funds must be paid back to the reserve account. The law suggests a one-year payback period but allows for temporary delays. Funds may be repaid from various sources such as lawsuit proceeds, loans, operating funds, or from special assessments in accordance with *Civil Code* §1365 and §1366.

Operating Budget

The operating budget is subject to a different set of considerations than reserves. This is where cash flow is most noticeable. With a zero-based operating budget as contemplated by §1366.1, loss of income or difficulty in assessment collections create serious concerns. Zero-basing the budget means that at the end of the year, if the pro forma budget estimates prove correct, the budget will be spent down to zero. As the monthly dues payments arrive, the reserve contribution is deducted and placed in the reserve account. The remaining funds should take care of the association's ongoing operating expenses.

When an unexpected operating expense comes up and an association borrows from reserves to meet short-term obligations there must be a specific plan to pay back and the plan and the reasons for borrowing must be reflected in the association's minutes. The law is very clear on this. It is in everyone's interest to preserve the ability of the association to meet long-term obligations. The amounts borrowed are expected to be paid back within one year unless the reason for delay is well-documented and reasonable.

Chapter 8 also addresses an association's ability to take a loan from the reserve fund as it deals with alternatives to special assessments such as bank loans.

If an association finds itself borrowing from reserves to meet operating expenses on a regular basis it could be an indication that the regular assessment is set too low. It may be time for an adjustment to the regular assessment or a special assessment to supplement the operating account. (See Chapter 8 for information on authority to specially assess.) Since the reserve contribution shouldn't be reduced without justification, and toying with reserves is discouraged by the legislature, a careful second look at operating funds may become necessary.

In cases where there is no prohibition in the governing documents on midyear increases, generally, regular assessments may be increased by the statutory limits of *Civil Code* §1366 up to 20 percent per year so long as proper notice is given (30 to 60 days before the assessment is imposed). If the increase is needed midyear the board should consult the association's attorney.

Remember that the budget is a tool, an estimate, it's flexible and not set in stone. The board should strive to achieve balance between income and expenses while meeting the ongoing needs of the association. If new and critical information indicating a need for more funds comes into play after the budget is circulated, there are legal remedies available to collect the necessary assessments.

A properly drawn operating budget allows for these fluctuations. Some CIDs create a contingency category and some figure monthly needs on the conservative (generous) side. When the air pump in the spa needs major, unplanned surgery to remove a small animal, or a special mailing becomes necessary, the directors often are able to find the needed extra money in the operating budget. There will almost certainly be unplanned expenses so it is better to allow a little extra something in the budget than to continually come up short.

Associations that have surplus operating funds at the end of the year can roll them over into the following year's budget. Rolling over operating funds should be authorized routinely with a vote at the annual membership meeting (or by written ballot) by approving a *resolution* that makes the leftover funds next year's income or rolls the excess into reserve accounts. This process avoids the funds being unfairly taxed as excess income (depending on how the association chooses to file). As a not-for-profit corporation, there should be no excess income on the association's books. If an association finds itself consistently rolling over more than a small amount, it should consider a dues reduction or take a serious look at the budgeting process.

KEY POINT
Associations must try to avoid assessing too high or too low. Good financial management requires an ongoing balancing act focused on collecting just the right amount.

Associations are not intended to be profit-making entities. The "nonprofit mutual benefit" corporate status and tax exemptions that apply are specially designed for CIDs. Income and corporate taxes on the association itself are minimal. Individual owners generally have a property tax liability to the county for the value of their unit, but the assessments they pay for maintenance of their home and the amenities are not taxable.

Losses

Associations experience losses, usually as a result of uncollectable assessments.

At the July meeting of the Heavenly HOA Board of Directors, officers of the association voted to write off two accounts that amounted to more than $4,000 in unpaid assessments.

"This is the first time we've had to do this," commented the vice president who had served on the board for ten years. "It looked like we had escaped the worst of the recessionary pressures until this happened."

The charge-offs were eventually accepted as reality, and the only way to clear the books of these bad debts.

"What makes it worse, is that we lose the money we had to pay our attorney too," said the president. "Normally, the person who does not pay assessments would be charged for legal fees incurred in collecting the debt. But when there is a lender foreclosure or bankruptcy or the person is judgment-proof, then we lose all the way around."

It is difficult for an association to avoid paying legal fees for collections since assertive collections often produce the best results. Tight procedural policies that are consistently followed help alleviate collection problems. Certain procedures should be followed from the first evidence that an account may have problems. Late notices and letters, liens and eventually a foreclosure or court judgment may have to be pursued.

There are disadvantages to both the association and the delinquent owner if established procedures are not invoked early on. For the owner, the debt may get too big to handle if it is ignored for long. For the association, if the collection procedures and timetable aren't followed, the debt may not be collectible. The timely filing of liens protects the association—to the extent such protection does any good—when an owner files bankruptcy. It shows up on any title search and this protects the association when a homeowner with an assessment debt tries to sell (through a conventional sale) or reappraise the property. If there is no lien and the owner sells the property to his Uncle Mutt, you can be sure Uncle will deny any responsibility for back dues. If the lien is in place, it is harder for anyone to deny that the money is owed and it leaves the association with more options.

What the write-off means to other homeowners at Heavenly HOA is that the $4,000 that would have been collected for association expenses (plus legal fees) has to come from somewhere else. That may result in increased assessments for those who have paid their bills in a responsible way. It's not fair—but it's life.

Yeah Ma, it's plum amazin'. They done up the budget without anyone endin' up dead.

Owners sometimes feel sorry for those whom the association goes after to collect a debt—until they realize the losses have to be made up out of their own pockets. Most associations will make some arrangement for homeowners who get behind to catch up by making extra payments so long as it isn't a prevailing problem. It is normally the homeowners who completely ignore their obligations to the association who you read about in the newspapers—those who lose their homes to assessment debt. They are the exception rather than the norm. But more commonly when an owner loses his home it is because he has stopped paying the association *and* the mortgage lender and the *lender* forecloses and takes the property.

Even when Heavenly HOA files a lien they stand in line behind the first mortgage holder on the property and any other lenders whose mortgages are recorded before the association's lien. So, as a practical matter, while filing the lien is important, the position of a CID is severely weakened when it comes to collecting overdue assessments on property where the mortgage is also in default. The tragedy is that dues-paying neighbors have to make up the difference.

KEY POINT
The losses incurred by a CID when any member fails to pay dues are made up by responsible association members who do pay.

Cost Controls

All owners have an interest in controlling costs of the association, to keep dues low as possible since dues are a factor in marketability. At the same time, maintaining the appearance and amenities of the property affect marketability as well.

Reserves? What reserves do you mean?

Clearly, these competing pressures weigh heavily on the people in charge. Cost minimization must be a high priority to all directors. That doesn't mean avoiding legitimate expenses or always going with the cheapest item or service offered. What it means is getting the *best value* for the dues dollar.

One place to look is at utilities. Gas, water, sewer, garbage and electricity are often big ticket items. High cost services should be first to be considered for review because that is where the greatest dollar savings can be found for a given percentage reduction. A simple way to save money is to evaluate services received for money spent. There are companies who audit utility usage and look for errors in billing and for on-site problems. They receive their fee as a portion of the money that they save for a CID, so it costs nothing to use such a service and could result in substantial savings.

Water

In California, water has always been an important issue and will continue to be, probably forever. CIDs can save on water and the often-linked sewer charges by installing low-flush toilets, monitoring landscape watering, or even replacing a water hungry landscape with drought-tolerant xeriscaping. Restricting water use is often necessary. Car washing may have to be limited or eliminated altogether during times of severe drought. Units with excessive water use may have to pay a premium or surcharge.

Depending on how the water is delivered to the units and who pays for it (owner or association), it may be necessary to install unit meters (known as "sub-meters") or take other actions against water wasters. Education is always the preferable choice— but education doesn't always work. Some people just don't care how their actions affect others.

Electricity

Many associations have been moving toward energy-efficient lighting, installing high pressure sodium security lighting and eliminating incandescent and fluorescent fixtures. Run cycles on spa and pool pumps and air conditioning can be adjusted to minimums. In common area rest rooms, timed or motion-sensing light switches can eliminate burning lights needlessly.

Gas and Solar Heat

Solar panels can augment gas heaters for swimming pools and can provide preheated water for a spa. Solar panels that have been in place for a number of years lose their efficiency as the dark paint on the collectors oxidizes and begins to reflect, rather than absorb, light. Simply repainting the collectors is claimed to improve efficiency by as much as 30 percent.

Efficiencies

Efficiencies can come from any number of areas. Heavenly HOA had the laborers working for their gardening service do simple repairs and replacement of broken sprinkler heads. They were able to stop using an expensive irrigation specialist and saved at least $8.00 on each sprinkler head repaired or replaced.

Changing the property damage insurance deductible from $500 to $2,000 per claim saved $3,400 a year, ten percent of Heavenly's *total* annual premium for all types of coverage. This deductible is often passed on to the individual homeowner's policy anyway, so it's worth considering.

By using preprinted coupon books, rather than monthly statements, and arranging with their bank to receive the monthly assessment checks directly for deposit, Heavenly HOA avoided management fees for preparing deposits and monthly billings.

Residents who have ideas for saving money should offer them to the directors for consideration. Brainstorming for efficiency works and the money saved is money that remains in your pocket.

CONDOGURU SPEAKS

Q: *I never use the swimming pool or spa. Why do I have to pay as much in dues as people who do?*

CONDOGURU: Good question. Now if I can only think up a good answer.... Oh, yeah, I remember. Most associations have a dues structure that is equal for all members. Some kinds of associations have a graduated scale of assessments based on such factors as the value or square footage of the individual unit or property.

Most CC&Rs have a *nonseverability* clause that says, in effect, that an owner *cannot reduce* his or her interest or obligation *by not using* a common amenity. It is the same as if you bought a single family home with a swimming pool. Whether you use the pool or not you still own it, maintain it and pay taxes on it.

In a condo the pool is part of the *value* of your property and contributes to the price when your unit sells.

If members were able to selectively avoid paying for this or that amenity, the association would be unable to count on needed income for maintenance and that would lower the value of everyone's unit.

If this answer makes you hot, go jump in the pool and cool down. After all, you paid for it.

Q: *My son has a gardening service, with his own darling little pickup truck and lawn mower and everything. How do I get him hired to mow the lawns? It is only right since we live here.*

CONDOGURU: I've seen your son's little pickup truck. It *is* darling and most of the time it's illegally parked.

Your association hires a professional gardening service that not only takes care of lawn mowing, but the full spectrum of maintenance, including water monitoring, fertilizing, dethatching, overseeding, irrigation system repairs and tree and shrub pruning. There is much more to the job than you might suspect.

There are a couple of approaches that your son might take to try for the contract. He could submit an unsolicited bid describing his education and ability and his company's history. The bid would have to convince the board of directors that he is capable of performing the job and has the proper liability insurance and workers compensation coverage and would have to give them a compelling reason to switch from the current contractor.

Or he could write a letter to the board asking for a bid package the next time the landscape job is open to competition.

If he gets the contract then he might have an excuse for parking his darling pickup on the lawn.

Q: *I had to pay a late fee. I don't think it's fair, I was only one day late. I have a good excuse. I was sleeping off a hangover.*

CONDOGURU: One day late is like almost on time or slightly pregnant. Late is late. The board of directors is obligated to operate the association as a business. To do otherwise would be a disservice to the rest of the homeowners. There is a legal reason for the late charge on dues. It works like this: If a payment of the monthly assessment is not received by the 15th of the month, a letter is automatically prepared and sent to the delinquent party (or party boy). The late fee usually just covers the administrative cost of the notice. The notice is a reminder to the homeowner but also serves to establish a date for any legal action that might later become necessary. If it happens that the second month's payment doesn't arrive, the account is turned over to our lawyer (the guy in the fluorescent green sharkskin suit) to take appropriate action. It is vital that each homeowner pays dues on time. If dues were not collected, the association would effectively cease to exist. Obligations of the association to pay for necessary services (like the guy with the darling pickup truck) don't go away.

But there is another point you need to understand. Your regular assessment was due the *first* day of the month. The grace period (during which you were late but no action was taken against you by the association) is until the 15th. When you don't pay until the 16th, you are not one day late, you are sixteen days late.

Q: *How come my monthly assessment seems to increase every year?*

CONDOGURU: The easy answer is *inflation*, but the Mighty Oracle of Truth (me) is never afraid to give the hard answer, so here goes. It is a combination of inflation and changing requirements that causes dues to rise. As an association ages, more expenses are incurred for routine repairs and replacement. The association directors play a guessing game each year and try to project what it will cost to run the place (operating budget) and to replace or renovate assets (reserve funds). They aren't supposed to assess too much or too little, but *just right*. Sounds like Baby Bear's porridge.

Budgets can be complicated and often depend on clairvoyance of the board. Directors consider previous budgets and reserve studies when determining assessment amounts. Serving on the board can be a real eye-opener as to the monetary needs of the association—why not try it? Even if you can't get elected, you can still attend board meetings and listen, or just sit back and eat your porridge—if it's *just right.*

Another alternative is to stick your head in the sand and complain, that's up to you, but think about the portion of your anatomy that will be above your head.

El Cid

Some owners try to get out of paying assessments by claiming an *offset*, such as, "My rain gutter didn't get cleaned this year, so I'm withholding dues." Owners, no matter how righteously indignant, should know that this is illegal. No one can withhold dues because they don't like something the board is doing or not doing. Owners need to consider this **before** they try the withholding game and end up with a lot of late fees and interest that they have to pay on the withheld dues.

CHAPTER 8

Paying For The Unexpected

Special Assessments and Borrowing

**What do you mean, I have to pay a special assessment
to finish the roofs? My roof is already finished.**

S imple words and phrases have been known to evoke strong
emotions in people—for politicians it may be *term limits,* for
writers *editorial control,* and for doctors *socialized medicine.* To homeowners in common interest developments, it could
well be *special assessments.*

Community association maintenance and administration is
paid for by homeowner assessments as discussed in Chapter 7. CID
operating budgets are formulated by considering expenses of the
association, income, and the necessity to fund reserve accounts.
Even with the best planning—which is not always the case since it
is often done by nonprofessionals—there are times when unexpected expenses arise and the association must look to its members
for additional funds. Ergo—the *special assessment.* A special assessment can be a homeowner's budget buster, especially in hard
financial times, as can any emergency requiring a substantial out-
pouring of cash. The owner of a single-family home may encounter

leaky roofs, construction defects, plumbing problems or simply have an end-of-the-month money shortage. A CID owner cannot expect to escape this completely.

A CID faces the same problems, but on a larger scale. Luckily, the number of owners, and therefore contributors, is also on a larger scale. The plus, of course, is that there is economy of scale when it comes to negotiating and paying for the work. When an unanticipated or unbudgeted expense arises, the board of directors is charged with solving the financial problem. They may decide to spend reserves, borrow money, wait a while, or poll the owners for a consensus before making a decision.

In a CID the board makes most of these decisions for the individual owners. Some people like being relieved of the responsibility for making difficult choices. That's one of the elements of "carefree living" that attracts them to CIDs. They don't have to budget, obtain bids, analyze the problem, or make any decisions—but they do need to be willing to pay for these advantages when the time comes.

Other owners do not like to be left out of the decision-making process and are known to complain if not consulted over substantial expenditures. Take for example, Joe, who wants each decision to be precisely right for his situation. He may decide he can live with a leaky roof or termites in the rafters for another year or two—or until he moves. He may feel comfortable with the risk of going without insurance. The directors in a common interest development do not have the luxury of choosing to do nothing—although if money isn't available to fix a problem it could turn out that way regardless.

Condo owners often have an expectation (that the courts sometimes adopt) that the board will take care of all association problems. Board members face the possibility of being taken to court if they procrastinate or fail to order necessary repairs or services or if they carelessly manage funds. Directors are fiduciaries—persons given a financial trust. Because of their responsibility for managing other peoples' money, more is expected of the directors than of an average Joe.

There is in law a "business judgment" standard that directors are expected to apply to their decisions. The standard calls for prudent decisions, made in good faith, and if necessary with the help of experts such as lawyers, CPAs or architects.

For owners who wish to have a hand in deciding association business matters, they can seize the opportunity by running for election to the board.

Special Assessments

Associations can levy special assessments to be paid in a single lump sum or in payments spread out over months or years, or they can have payment deferred until a later date. *Civil Code* §1366 (b) sets limits on imposing special assessments. CC&Rs may address or limit the amount of a special assessment that can be levied by the board of directors but the law controls. It says the board of directors may not make special assessments totaling more than 5 percent of the association's budgeted gross expenses for the fiscal year without approval of the membership, unless there is an emergency. These rules apply to special assessments imposed on everyone, not individual compliance or special purpose assessments as authorized by some CC&Rs. Emergency circumstances (as authorized by *Civil Code* §1366) include court-ordered assessments, repairs to correct safety hazards, or extraordinary expenses that could not have reasonably been foreseen when the budget was devised. When membership approval is required for a special assessment, it takes approval of a *majority of a quorum* of the homeowners (counting a quorum as 51%) under *Civil Code* §1366.

Regardless of the reason for a special assessment or increase in regular assessments, all owners have to be notified by first class mail, between 30 and 60 days before the first payments come due (§1366 (c)). The association has power under the law to collect assessments as well as any costs that might be involved in the collection—including reasonable attorney fees (§1366 (d)).

KEY POINT

When needed *to meet emergencies,* special assessments of more than 5 percent of the annual budget may be levied by the board of directors without approval of the membership.

Boards also have the power to impose late charges and interest for late payments. The late fees are capped at $10 or 10 percent of the delinquency, whichever is greater (unless the CC&Rs state a smaller late fee) and as much as 12 percent annual interest (§1366 (d)).

Failure by a homeowner to pay a special assessment can be devastating to an association and the delinquent homeowner as well, as was discussed in Chapter 7. The directors have little choice but to pursue collection, even via the courts, to protect the other homeowners and the integrity of the CID. If they do not take reasonable steps to collect they, themselves, could be at risk for failure to fulfill their fiduciary duties.

Alternatives To Special Assessments

In California, boards have some latitude in making spending and funding decisions. They may legally increase *regular* assessments (dues) up to 20 percent per year without a vote of the owners, and/or impose special assessments in the amount of 5 percent of the budgeted gross expenses for any given fiscal year without approval of the membership. They may borrow from reserves in some cases. They may look for ways to supplement income over the long term or short term or to offset expenses. They may consider borrowing to meet unexpected expenses or fund capital improvements. In other words, there are alternatives to raising the dues. Let's look at some more creative ways to raise extra money to fix that crack just discovered in the swimming pool.

Some directors find that facing their neighbors with a special assessment tests their courage and intelligence. Many would consider taking a long vacation—if they didn't need the money to pay their share of the special assessment.

Single-family homeowners facing a cracked pool and empty pockets might set their kids up in a lemonade stand on the sidewalk, take on an extra job, turn to weekly garage sales or dispose of their treasures at a flea market for the extra cash. CIDs differ. Because of their non-profit mutual benefit corporation status, they have no product or service to sell. Revenue sources are limited. Some CIDs seek to augment their treasury by leasing some of their amenities to nonresidents to offset costs. Some collect fees for neighborhood use of the swimming pool (once the crack is fixed, of course); some offer their clubhouse for nonmember wedding receptions, community meetings, etc. A few resort to organized functions such as on-site bake sales or talent contests to fatten the bank account. A CID might host a fund raiser to deal with the pool crack—an alternative that might seem preferable to special assessments. Such fund raisers are staples of churches, clubs and schools. They appear to be innocent, reasonable, eminently workable solutions, right?

Unfortunately, the really creative CIDs could find themselves on shaky ground if they raise revenue from outside the assessments. Nonprofit mutual benefit corporations have defined requirements as to what portion of their income is nontaxable—regular and special assessments for the most part. Their nonprofit corporate status, which entitles them to important tax benefits, may come into question if significant income is derived from other sources. (And the answer is *yes*—CIDs do have to file tax returns.)

Liability exposure, another potentially serious consequence, is increased when the outside world is invited onto CID property. Some liability insurance policies specifically exclude organized group activities that are not connected to association members.

Compliance with federal and state civil rights and antidiscrimination statutes requiring special access and accommodation for disabled people (when the public is invited in) may end up costing an association more than it's worth to allow nonmember use of facilities. There are stringent penalties that may be imposed for failure to comply with federal antidiscrimination regulations and statutes such as the *Federal Fair Housing Amendments of 1988* (FFHA), the *Americans with Disabilities Act* (ADA), and the *Unruh Civil Rights Act*—the California antidiscrimination statute.

KEY POINT

Nonprofit mutual benefit homeowner association corporations are limited in the nontaxable income they may earn from outside sources without jeopardizing their non-profit status.

There are other potential negatives to sharing facilities with the public. Association members shouldn't have to compete with outsiders for use of their commonly-owned amenities. So it is best, generally, to look for other answers to the funding question.

Getting a Bank Loan
A Real-Life Story

Since legislators are tightening up on reserve borrowing by imposing new laws almost yearly, associations must look elsewhere to find funding for emergency or unbudgeted items. Bank loans are now more readily available than they were only a few years ago—possibly due to the huge need that arose following the Northridge earthquake. CIDs faced massive, immediate expenses for rebuilding. Some banks stepped in to meet those emergency needs. As a result, they found that even an association hit hard by the earthquake could still be a prudent risk. Those banks generally found association loans to be profitable and, as a result, more lending institutions are opening their doors to associations. These loans make sense because even if one or several homeowners falter, the rest will likely carry the association through the repayment cycle.

Let's take a look at a real-life example at one of our favorite pieces of real estate—Nirvana Homeowner Association.

SITUATION: The association is a 15-year old, 200-unit condominium complex with 25 residential buildings and a clubhouse. The roofs, wood shingles over spaced sheathing, are in poor condition. The manager is receiving an average of ten calls for leaks during each rain. Repair and maintenance budgets are taking a beating just paying for the band-aid repairs that are necessary to avoid further expenses from rain damage.

RESERVES INADEQUATE: The roof replacement reserve contribution from regular dues is $5,000 per month and the balance of $350,000 in the reserves falls far short of the estimated cost of reroofing, which is $700,000. Considering all reserve categories together there is still not enough money to fund reroofing. It's clear that new roofs are needed *well before* enough reserve money has accumulated.

The directors of Nirvana Homeowner Association were nervous. Their *own* roofs were beginning to leak. When the handyman walked on top of the buildings fixing leaks, he caused more leaks as shingles split under his weight.

One unit had to be reroofed on an emergency basis so escrow could close. Visions of multi-thousand dollar lawsuits danced heavily in the heads of board members faced with solving the problem.

How do we pay for this project? they wondered, lying awake, hoping to lose the next election.

One director did some homework: he studied the situation, made inquiries and laid out the choices to the others.

"We could choose to do nothing at the moment and wait until the reserves are sufficient—about five and a half years. We could start reroofing now with the funds we have and, moving slowly, finish in five and a half years. But if we choose either of these options somebody is going to have to wait five and a half years for a roof that needs replacing *now*. And what if the materials we start with are not available in the same color in five years? Besides, all the roofs are in such poor shape that it would be impossible to determine which ones to do first. They *all* need to be first.

"The third and only option that will prevent a mass lynching of us directors is to begin reroofing immediately."

"Yes, but..." said Jimmy Tightwad, the treasurer (who *always* said, yes, but....), "...how do you plan to pay for it without touching other reserves, Mr. Panty Smarts."

"That's Mr. *Smarty Pants,*" said Mr. Smarty Pants, the smartest of all the directors. "We have a couple of options. One: special assess each homeowner $1750 and run for cover. Two: wait for the money to accumulate and hide out for five and a half years.

Or three, get a roof renovation loan for $250,000 and finish the job in a year and a half. During the reroofing period about $100,000 would accumulate in roof reserves to make up the $350,000 needed under the current bid."

The others gasped in disbelief at such a proposal.

"Wouldn't payments take a special assessment?" asked one.

"Plus we'd have to pay interest," said another.

"Neither borrower nor lender be," cried still another.

"WRONG," boomed Mr. Smarty Pants (who occasionally liked to boom for effect), silencing the room. "**No** special assessments. **No** increase in dues, and **no** angry mob." He outlined the plan he had previously discussed with the association's banker.

In this case, the association had already earmarked $5,000 per month to pay for roofs by putting that much into the reserve funds. That money would simply be redirected to loan repayment. The loan meant the difference between new roofs now or new roofs much later—with mayhem against the directors in the near future.

Association members had the right to vote on the contract (which banks usually require even if the CC&Rs don't), so the directors explained to the homeowners that the loan would not be an additional burden—that it was secured by future income from dues—and that no property would be encumbered. The vote was taken after explanations to the homeowners through a series of newsletter articles and informational meetings.

The balloting results were 95 percent *yes* votes, one *no* vote and a few abstentions. That was a year and a half ago. Now there are 200 new roofs at Nirvana, the repair and maintenance budget is on track, and the directors sleep better than they have in years.

And they all lived happily ever after—until someone noticed termites in the clubhouse rafters and that nasty crack in the swimming pool.

CONDOGURU

SPEAKS

**Borrowing
From Reserves**

Q: *Why special assess? Why not just go to reserves and take a little cash out for a while until things even out. Just let it build back up. It'll be painless. Look, I've got a kitchen remodeling planned and if there is a special assessment for the roofs, then I'll have to cancel.*

CONDOGURU: There is absolutely no question about the *attractiveness* of such a plan to avoid special assessments. That's why the California Legislature has placed severe restrictions on an association's ability to rob Peter—Paul doesn't always seem to get around to paying him back. The reserves tend not to *just naturally build up* before the board faces its next crisis that, coincidentally, could be solved with another dip into the reserves. It takes courage to look your neighbors in the eye while going for their wallets— especially if it is because, as a director, you weren't clairvoyant. The quality of mercy is truly tested by special assessments.

In 1995, *The Davis-Stirling Act* was amended to place much tighter restrictions on reserve borrowing than were previously in effect. The stringent requirements for these loans will force many CIDs to look for alternate funding methods. The law now requires:

- Loans from reserves to be repaid within one year (any delays must be temporary).

- The board to make a finding that explains the reason for borrowing and the plan to repay. The finding must be in writing and recorded in the minutes.
- Any special assessment to pay off the loan requires homeowner approval in accordance with *The Davis-Stirling Act.*
- Notice to members.
- An accounting of litigation expenses be done at least quarterly and made available for inspection by members.

El Cid

What is said is true—the legislators don't like to see associations borrow from reserves so they keep tightening the rules. One of the hottest controversies is over borrowing from reserves to fund litigation for construction defect lawsuits. Some attorneys interpret *Civil Code* §1365 to allow use of reserves for construction defect litigation. Others consider the use of reserve funds for construction defect litigation to be subject to the "borrowing" rules. If there is a need to specially assess owners to pay back reserves, there is now a requirement that the homeowners approve that special assessment.

The directors meant only to rob Peter to pay Paul,
but ended up mugging their victim and
leaving him in critical condition.

CHAPTER 9

Insurance

How much insurance do I need?
I thought the association bought insurance.

In the minds of many, the subject of insurance conjures an image of a sales representative setting up his display board among magazines on the coffee table. He speaks in a funereal voice, "If, *God forbid*, something should happen to either of you then the other would collect...." Life insurance isn't the subject of this chapter, but residents of a CID can find their lives dramatically changed by the insurance they buy—or fail to buy.

As odious a subject as insurance can be, you can't afford to be ignorant about it. Associations need certain types of insurance. Each owner also faces obligations and risks that only insurance or substantial personal wealth can protect against. Owners should carry insurance to protect them against loss of their personal property, improvements they have made to their homes that are not covered by the association's policy, and liability for accidents inside their homes. Tenants renting in a CID need personal property and liability insurance too.

Agents offering insurance for owners of condominium or PUD properties need special expertise. They should know the details of how this coverage differs from other types of property and liability coverage and be able to read and understand CC&Rs so they can write the proper kind of policy. The insurance carried by the association bears on the coverage needed by individual homeowners.

It is unlikely that anyone severely shaken by the 1994 Northridge earthquake would ignore the insurance issue. They know, firsthand, what can happen when there are misconceptions about insurance coverage. Entire associations have been disbanded, and homes lost, because of inadequate insurance.

Association Insurance

As mentioned, the association must carry insurance, and homeowners need it too. Let's first consider the insurance that an association must or should carry. As a minimum, there are four general insurance coverages that the association needs: liability, property damage, directors and officers (D&O), and fidelity. An association generally should carry workers compensation and special coverages such as for earthquake damage repair. It is helpful to have a general understanding of exactly what the association's insurance policies cover so that homeowners can then determine the insurance they need to provide for themselves.

General Liability. Most everyone is familiar with general liability insurance. It is somewhat similar to the PL & PD (public liability and property damage) found commonly in automobile insurance. This coverage is essential for the CID. It protects the association and its owner members from claims for an accident, injury, or damage to property. It could be for a common area mishap or some action of the association by its members, directors, residents, guests, employees or agents. It usually provides money for defense if the association is sued for an injury or property damage claim. It should not be confused with directors and officers (D&O) liability coverage which relates more to *specific acts* of the board of directors or officers. If the claim is because of specific acts of the board or an individual director or officer the D&O coverage, described below, would apply instead.

I told John that I wouldn't go on a carriage ride with him unless he could insure my safety. He assured me that he had liability insurance because he was liable to do anything.

Most governing documents require liability coverage of at least $1 million. Because of *Civil Code* §1365.9, added in 1995, many associations are increasing the amount of their general liability and D&O coverage to at least $2 or $3 million. (The D&O requirement may be removed by the legislature.) That code section does not *require* the higher amounts, but it provides protection for individual homeowners in some associations (mostly condos) from being sued or held personally liable for an accident in the common area if those minimum amounts of insurance are carried by the association—$2 million for associations with 100 or fewer owners and $3 million for those with more than 100 owners.

A claim made by a person who falls in the common area or is hurt using the recreational facilities is normally passed on to the association's general liability insurance carrier. A claim for an accident inside someone's unit should be made against the unit owner's policy. Unless the cause can be attributed to the association in some way, it will probably be the individual's problem, not the association's because the owner has full control inside the unit. If there is an accident in an exclusive use common area (as defined in Chapter 1) a question could arise as to whose insurance would apply, the association's or the owner's. Since the exclusive use area is maintained and controlled by the owner, responsibility for the accident might fall to the owner. On the other hand, the association may be sued—it depends on the details of the case. Homeowners are wise to have the extra protection of individual liability coverage and not rely on the association's policy as complete protection. Along with liability coverage, homeowners should obtain "loss assessment" insurance (described more fully below) to protect them from special assessments that might be imposed by the association in the event of a claim against the association.

Property Damage. Associations must insure against property damage to commonly owned real and personal property for hazards such as fire. In some cases flood or earthquake insurance is required—as discussed below.

In a condominium the members generally own the buildings as tenants-in-common and the association's "master" policy covers those buildings. In a planned unit development (PUD) the members usually own their individual lots and all the structures built on the lots. In this case, the PUD owners should have individual coverage for damage to the structures that contain their homes, because the association's policy would cover only the common area buildings and property that is owned by the association. When the clubhouse burns down or other commonly-owned property is damaged, the association's property damage policy would usually pay the costs to rebuild. In cases where multi-unit residential buildings (not just interior air space) are owned by the owners, the association's master coverage would normally rebuild damaged buildings and original fixtures, but in most cases would not pay for any furnishings or expensive wall or floor coverings. In other words, the association's policy would restore the building to its original condition without costly improvements that have been made by the owners. In some cases, the insurance proceeds may be used to paint and carpet also but probably won't cover "top-of-the-line" paint or carpet. In many instances, associations, their insurance companies, and the owners have disputes over the extent of covered items. A clear understanding of master policy coverage limits will help owners choose wisely in personal insurance requirements.

Directors and Officers. Some call this *dumb decision defense.* Mostly, it is used to defend the directors and officers and the association in court cases where lawsuits are filed alleging breach of fiduciary duty (a variation of negligent behavior) and may be used to pay damages if the association loses. A claim might also be made for the board's failure to enforce the CC&Rs or to buy enough insurance. Failure to insure adequately is usually listed as a *specific exclusion* to D&O covered items so deciding not to purchase required insurance is one bonehead decision a board mustn't make.

D&O insurance is most often conditional on the directors acting in a good-faith manner within their capacity as board members, as opposed to taking individual, intentionally malicious action in a certain situation. The board should clarify the details of coverage with the carrier. For example, some policies may exclude coverage for committee members who aren't *elected* board members, while some allow coverage for committee members.

A director who abuses power and intentionally causes harm can expect the association's D&O carrier to either refuse coverage or provide it along with a "reservation of rights" which enables the insurance carrier to come back to the director, if it is later determined the act was outside covered actions, and demand reimbursement for defense costs and for damages paid. All associations should have D&O coverage. If the association cannot get it, then the individuals serving may be able to get coverage to protect themselves through their homeowners policy for service on a nonprofit board. Coverage for board acts is important to both the association and those serving as directors or officers.

Fidelity Bonding. This coverage protects the association from losses in the event a director or employee with access to association funds suddenly takes a vacation in a country that does not have an extradition treaty with the United States.

Workers Compensation. The circumstances of each CID will dictate whether workers compensation should be carried. Knowledgeable legal advisors or insurance providers should be consulted about the need for this type of insurance. If the CID has employees or volunteers who work for the association, workers compensation insurance is required for their protection. Even if there are no employees, minimal limits of workers compensation insurance should be considered to protect the board members who administer or inspect the property. Workers compensation insurance also proves important if an independent contractor is hired who has employees but no workers compensation coverage. If an employee of that contractor is hurt on a job, the association may be liable to pay for the injuries if it has no workers compensation insurance.

Personal Insurance for Homeowners

Loss Assessment. One of the most valuable, least understood, and most overlooked forms of insurance is loss assessment coverage. It is not available to associations, but homeowners in CIDs can, and should, purchase it in amounts equal to the potential risks. Loss assessment coverage may be used to pay special assessments imposed on homeowners in CIDs. Loss assessment coverage is designed to apply to assessments imposed in the event an award or judgment against the association exceeds its coverage; to a deductible payment for property damage; or costs to rebuild common areas or structures which are damaged and for which there is not enough insurance money available—which could happen in a major fire. Loss assessment coverage for this excess liability or property damage is normally offered as part of a residential property policy in minimal limits of coverage ($1,000-$2,500). Additional coverage is most often available at a very low rates.

Earthquake Loss Assessment. This coverage is purchased separately from the property or liability loss assessment coverage described above. This policy rider covers special assessments for earthquake damage to common areas and jointly-owned structures.

Personal Liability and Property Damage. CID homeowners who do not maintain personal insurance policies risk financial ruin in the case of large liability settlements against them in actions separate from the association. Without adequate property insurance there is the risk of losing personal possessions, and expensive improvements like parquet flooring or fabric wallpaper. Association insurance does not cover these items or relocation costs for displaced homeowners or loss of income from displaced tenants.

Earthquake Insurance Coverage

Earthquake Insurance. There is no current state requirement for CIDs to carry earthquake insurance. At the time of this writing (early 1995) earthquake insurance is not readily available for associations or owners. Earthquake insurance will continue to be a concern for California CIDs. When they can get it, it's very expensive and the deductibles are high. When they can't get it, they risk an owners' ability to sell or refinance because some lenders require it before underwriting the loans. CIDs continue to be at the mercy of insurance companies and mortgage lenders who jockey to limit their liability.

A major secondary mortgage market provider, the Federal Home Loan Mortgage Corporation—commonly called Freddie Mac—rocked the condo industry in early 1995. Freddie Mac imposed guidelines requiring earthquake coverage *and* prefunding or insurance coverage for *deductibles* on California condominium developments. As a result, many mortgage lenders will require proof of association earthquake insurance before lending to individual owners in years to come. There will almost certainly be significant changes in the way earthquake coverage is obtained and applied. Following the Northridge earthquake, with huge losses to area CIDs and to the insurance and banking industries, many large providers have stopped writing coverage altogether. Before the Northridge earthquake in 1994, most associations and individuals who had earthquake insurance felt secure their coverage was adequate. That view, and a lot else, changed after Northridge.

Earthquake Coverage and How it Works

Most earthquake policies held by CIDs and individuals have a 10 percent deductible. Some insurance companies are requiring deductibles as high as 25 percent. Having to pay for 10 percent of the damages does not sound too bad except that the 10 percent deductible is not figured on the total damages. Rather, it is based on the total amount of the coverage. In some policies it relates to the *first* 10 percent of the *scheduled* replacement value for each building. The scheduled replacement value is the estimate of complete rebuilding costs used to set premiums.

Let's look at how a typical policy of earthquake insurance would work on a totally destroyed four-unit building at Nirvana HOA, an earthquake-insured condominium association.

Assume the scheduled (and actual) replacement cost of the building is $200,000. The first 10 percent ($20,000) would be the association's responsibility (the deductible). Insurance would pay the remaining $180,000. Market value of the four units is not considered in the calculation.

Let's say that a second building identical to the first had less damage and the building could be repaired for $40,000. The association pays $4,000 (10 percent) and the insurance carrier picks up the other $36,000, right? *Wrong!*

Since the deductible applies to the *scheduled replacement* cost for each building, the association would have to pay the *same deductible* as on the totally destroyed building—$20,000. On the building with minor damage insurance would cover the remaining $20,000. So on this building, practically applied, the deductible is **50 percent**. If the *actual* replacement cost exceeds the *scheduled* replacement cost, insurance covers the higher amount up to *policy limits*.

Both earthquakes and earthquake insurance are a gamble. Even CIDs like Nirvana HOA that have an appropriate amount of insurance could still face a hefty repair bill following a devastating earthquake. Costs not covered by insurance would have to be funded by special assessments—this is when homeowners who were wise enough to purchase earthquake loss assessment coverage congratulate themselves on being so smart.

Earthquake insurance? Not for me, old chap.
When the Big One hits, I cut the rope.

All members of this condominium association face equal responsibility in this case. Complete destruction of one building and minor damage to another do not alter the owners' overall obligations. This is because each owner has an equal, indivisible, nonseverable share in the common property. The essence of a mutual benefit common interest association is *shared benefits balanced by a sharing of the risks.* In a PUD, however, each building owner may be individually responsible for earthquake insurance and rebuilding. The association may have insurance on the common area structures to the extent there are any, such as a clubhouse, in which case everyone, again, would share in the risks and obligations. Some PUDs which are made up of multiunit buildings will have an association master policy covering the buildings (similar to condominium associations).

Higher earthquake insurance deductibles of at least 20 to 25 percent will likely be the norm in California in future years. Premiums can be expected to increase because of the magnitude of the risk which cannot be ignored after Northridge, and the limited number of carriers willing to take that risk. Even if a statewide program of coverage (such as the California FAIR Plan) continues to offer coverage including that for earthquakes, the cost will still probably be difficult to swallow considering the limited coverage in such a plan. There may be little choice in the future but for associations to procure coverage whatever the cost. If the lenders won't lend without it, it will become a business routine, just as property hazard insurance coverage is now. There will, no doubt, be increased pressure to raise homeowner monthly dues to cover the higher earthquake premiums.

CONDOGURU SPEAKS

I have nothing to add.

El Cid

That's a first!

PART 3

RUNNING THE RANCH

CHAPTER 10   ASSOCIATION MANAGEMENT

CHAPTER 11   THE ROLE OF VOLUNTEERS

CHAPTER 10

Association Management

Who are those clowns?

Homeowner associations are created to fulfill and oversee the functions of management, administration and day-to-day operations for common interest developments. They are run by boards of directors elected by the homeowners. The CC&Rs refer to the association created to manage each development and there is reference in California law to the entities called *community associations.* The association's bylaws set up the organizational structure and direct how the board members are elected.

Many times community (homeowner) associations and boards of directors take a beating both at home and in the press but there is little interest from the press in the thousands of well-run associations—except, of course, in the real estate ads in your Sunday newspaper that promise carefree living.

At times, associations take a beating in the courts as well. Serving as a director can be thankless, but willing souls take up the challenge. Some associations have a tough time filling board positions; others have heavy competition for board vacancies.

From a director's perspective, service can involve tedium, hours of research, weekend training, hard decisions and a bushel basket full of criticism. Why would anyone want to work under such conditions? Talk to a director who cares about the association and you'll detect pride and self-satisfaction in the service he or she gives. For directors, a problem solved, a renovation project completed or a tough decision that turns out well is exhilarating.

For some directors the satisfaction of controlling the future of the property and the fate of their community is the incentive that draws them to service. To be part of the management team can have a strong attraction. Certainly, there are individuals who are less than altruistic in their desire to serve—one-issue candidates, those with a grudge, or those who merely want the power and recognition that come with the office.

If the majority of CID owners (who are content to allow others to serve) were asked what they knew about the board it's unlikely they would have an answer. The board, to many, is invisible. There is little recognition that anyone does anything to keep the ship afloat—until disaster strikes. Few owners care or question how the association operates. Some may never attend a meeting, read a newsletter, volunteer, or even speak out. For the most part these owners are in it for the "carefree" living.

A few, in relation to the numbers living in CIDs, find pleasure in nit-picking board actions, criticizing decisions. Just as most every town has its "character" who bedevils the city council there is usually at least one malcontent in every CID. Dealing with their distractions successfully can test the patience of the best directors—especially when the malcontent gets elected to the board, though at times the experience changes his attitude for the better.

There are situations, of course, where the board is not operating very well and the local "malcontent" may just be someone who has noticed the problem and has become vocal about it. Deciding whether it is an incompetent board or a community nut that is the problem may take some outside help in the form of an association management consultant.

KEY POINT
The main problem with directors and managers is that they are recruited from the human race.
—*Condoguru*

In the case of an incompetent or malicious director, or board, owners can band together to put pressure on the board for reforms, as discussed in Chapter 5. Boards have power to make decisions, establish rules and sue (owners as well as others) using association funds. This makes the board very powerful and when this power is mixed with abusive tendencies the result can ruin an association financially and politically. Abuse of power coupled with owner apathy can dramatically stifle the efforts of a conscientious owner who has detected a problem. Directors acting in concert, or a single director with the personal power to sway the rest according to his or her will, are the stuff of news stories. Unchecked power in the hands of an abusive board or its most controlling member can lead to an uprising of the membership. By the time this happens, substantial resources are at stake and significant damage may have already been done.

Courts have different ways of looking at CIDs and their boards. Some courts call community associations "mini-governments" likening them to city governments. This perception exists because the boards are elected by the owners—like a city council—and there is often a managing agent and service providers—like a city manager and city service staff. The CC&Rs are like zoning restrictions and city ordinances and the governing documents, taken together, read much like a city charter. These courts hold that since CIDs operate like governments, the board members are like public servants, with a *fiduciary duty* to all residents (owners and nonmember tenants), including the *duty to enforce* the CC&Rs.

Detractors, ignorant of a director's huge responsibilities, may think of them as mere clowns with big sticks.

Some judges second guess a board's decisions to see whether its duty was fulfilled to the satisfaction of the court's *after-the-fact* review. Some courts try to apply federal and state constitutions to associations and in doing so create a "government official" standard for the volunteer directors. By this reasoning volunteer directors face the same obligations as paid government officials without the protection from lawsuit that government officials enjoy when they serve.

Enlightened courts draw at least two distinct and meaningful differences between governments and CIDs. From the governance point of view, cities are *public*; and common interest developments are *private* entities, usually corporations. Taking the homeowner's point of view, the courts identify the second difference as "consensual participation." Citizens of a city, county, state and country have little choice but to accept government regulations. These same citizens have a choice in purchasing homes in CIDs—a choice to live in that particular place for their own reasons. They *voluntarily* subject themselves to additional restrictions of the CC&Rs by *consent*.

Other courts use the "business judgment rule" to analyze association actions, giving more deference to board decisions and upsetting them only when there was clear abuse of power or discretion. But treating associations as businesses also can subject them to antidiscrimination laws which require admittance of all groups and special accommodations for the disabled.

KEY POINT

CIDs are different than city governments because membership is voluntary and homeowners may drop out by selling their property, an option not offered by government.

Still other courts compare boards to landlords, holding them to an even more difficult standard of care to make the development safe and protect the homeowners' well being. Courts have found board members personally liable in some cases for failure to make the development crime-safe for residents. These court decisions are the kind that make directors most nervous. These courts would have CID boards accept a *social responsibility* for their citizens in addition to the contractual obligation that arises from the CC&Rs.

Management By Directors

The roles of the directors and association officers are clearly defined in the CC&Rs and bylaws, or they should be. The directors are uncompensated volunteers who take on responsibility for what is in many cases a multimillion-dollar corporation. They are charged with administration and management of the CID, including day-to-day and long-range operations and policy. There are myriad laws in California that direct the board's actions and pile on even more responsibilities that often go far beyond what association documents suggest. Anything the association is charged to do by contract or law must be directed by the board. The laws relating to community associations apply to all but a few CIDs no matter what their size or financial magnitude.

Directors are responsible for decisions needed to keep the organization operating and viable. The board normally has authority to hire a professional manager, though bylaws may require a vote of the owners or may limit the term of any contract to one year or less. The board may delegate duties to the manager, but it cannot delegate responsibility for its decisions—since it retains ultimate responsibility a wise board maintains a *check and balance* system. Giving a manager too much authority without the requisite controls can result in very big problems. Conscientious managers will not accept authority for making the broad and sweeping policy decisions that should rightfully be made by the board.

A board must not avoid its own duty to review bank reconciliations and income and expense records—at least quarterly under *Civil Code* §1365—and to review the reserve study annually (§1365.5). The board cannot escape responsibility for sending the requisite pro forma budget, reserve information and mandatory legal disclosures to the membership, though it may appoint the manager to do the actual work. Nor can the board avoid fiduciary responsibilities related to prudent money management although it may delegate task functions to the manager. It may accept recommendations from the manager who has access to helpful resources or expertise that the board does not have. The board may rely on a managing agent to record minutes of meetings and advise on parliamentary procedure but it *cannot* delegate holding meetings to the manager and fail, itself, to meet.

Management of a community association encompasses facets of both business and government including conducting open and closed session meetings, accounting for and distributing financial and other information to members, reviewing reserve components and funding, hiring contractors and employees and reviewing operations.

Because of the level of activity and expertise required to successfully and legally operate a CID, many associations will hire managing agents and professionals in the fields where help is needed.

Managing Agents

A paid manager might be employed directly by the association or through a management company. They may work on-site or off-site, and may be an associate or the principal in a professional management company. Varying levels of authority are delegated to the manager—usually on a sliding scale in relation to direct involvement by the board. In other words, the less hands-on involvement by the board, the more authority given to the manager. Minimal manager involvement might include accounting functions or day-to-day operations. It is most often the manager, not the directors, who responds initially to owner complaints, oversees contractors, arranges for mailing meeting notices, and provides financial information and disclosures to members. Managers often communicate directly with owners regarding assessment collections and violations of the governing documents.

Some associations have left managing agents completely to their own devices without an established review process and have been sorry after funds were discovered missing. Managers have a stake in efficient operation of the property—it's their livelihood. Most also have a strong interest in keeping a good reputation. It is in a manager's best interest to stay honest since word quickly gets around the local CIDs.

Sometimes one or more board members are paid to perform certain management tasks for the association. While this arrangement has sometimes proven effective for some associations, most legal professionals will advise against it. Most associations that use this practice do not bother with a formal employee or contractor arrangement (such as a written contract) and the practice remains "loosey-goosey" until a problem arises. And the potential for problems is high. A director's participation in decision-making involving his or her paid duties is improper. Even when a paid director abstains from votes that may affect personal compensation and makes all of the necessary disclosures, owners may object once they learn of the arrangement. Suspicions run high when directors get paid, especially when a dissident homeowner finds out that a director or his relative is being paid for services to the association. Regardless of whether there is impropriety, the mere perception by owners of director self-dealing can embroil a board in controversy, put it on the defensive, and divert its attention from business.

The compensated director board member may find the protections of *Civil Code* §1365.7, which provides immunity from lawsuit for volunteer board members who serve *without compensation*, in jeopardy. Some associations allow a full or partial dues waiver for directors. An association considering this concept should seek legal counsel. Such an arrangement will probably require homeowner approval and may engender legal problems.

What Qualifications Are Required for a Manager?

This question stirs much controversy. For years there has been a push in California to require licensing for property managers. Some states mandate manager licensing and add a continuing education requirement. California does not. If the board or its members are performing management tasks, there is no current published statewide standard of competency for them to reference. There is no mandatory training for directors, much to the chagrin of some in the industry. Some industry groups adopted standards of ethics and articulated them. It is probably fair to say those managers who offer in their resume experience *plus* educational certification have more expertise, as would be the case in any profession.

If a board member who has related expertise—a CPA-director, for example, who offers financial advice to the board—that director will likely be held to a higher legal standard of care than other nonexpert directors. The standard of care a board member must exercise is intensified when he or she is a CPA, attorney, architect or other professionally qualified person. A director-professional offering advice to the rest of the board members has, in that instance, arguably stepped out of the role of director and into the role of professional. The question of whether the advice was given for monetary compensation may well have little effect on exposure to liability.

Directors must be very careful about exactly how much exposure they create for themselves. California *Corporations Code* §7231 provides some legal protection for directors of incorporated associations, which most in California are, who act in good faith and consult knowledgeable experts for matters outside their own expertise. Using outside experts is a safer way to go—but certainly costs and savings are factors to consider if special expertise is available on the board.

Some tasks are considered outside the scope of the manager's duties.

KEY POINT

Directors who are industry professionals
need to be careful when offering advice
to their own boards to avoid losing
protection the law offers
to volunteer directors.

Managers and professional managing agents may not have to be licensed as such but they are subject to certain legal requirements. Under *Civil Code* §1363.2 they must disclose any licenses—such as real estate—or professional designations they may hold—to association boards. If disciplinary action has occurred under those licenses, that has to be revealed too. They have to provide names of the business principals and the form of business entity (sole proprietorship, partnership, "S" corporation, etc.). They are not to commingle association funds with their own or those of other associations except in specific cases. A manager may "pass-through" money using a holding account for receipts and payment of expenses if the accounting practice was established before 1990.

Even without formal licensing, managers have fiduciary responsibility to associations, just as board members do, but as stated earlier, standards for managers are industry-driven. Just about anyone can hang out a shingle declaring himself a property manager. Some of the industry groups provide training and continuing education for managers and directors. Managers may work toward designations that attest to their expertise. This training does not go unnoticed. Unlike bad news which tends to travel like lightning through the industry, the good education and reputation of a competent, ethical manager travels slowly so it is in the interest of all managers to maintain a polished, professional image. A few unethical or outright crooked operators exist, as they do in any industry, but they usually don't last long.

Training Opportunities

Education is the foundation upon which success is built. More, it is the lubrication a community association needs for smooth operation of the corporation and understanding between directors and managers. Managers and directors should view education as an ongoing process that includes professional seminars, review of industry publications and membership in organizations that offer up-to-date information through regular functions. There are several groups that offer education for homeowners, board members and managers. We have listed a few of these organizations active in California in the Appendix.

A manager's or director's responsibility is broad, encompassing all aspects of a corporation. It is only with proper training and an appreciation for the full scope of authority that either can do the job well. And their performance is vital to the financial, political and mental health of the CID.

CONDOGURU

SPEAKS

Q: *I've seen a lot of bad press on condominium associations. What's going on?*

CONDOGURU: It's a conspiracy by the fourth estate to give the ol' Guru a conniption. Actually, common interest developments are easy targets for negative press coverage. There are a couple of reasons for this. One is that a few homeowners want to avoid CC&R restrictions and wave the flag of *personal liberty* while attempting to paint the association as an evil, oppressive empire run by the Nazis (i.e., board of directors and manager). You wouldn't think that Nazis had the time to run a CID.

Another reason, and this is the most tragic, is that there *are* some associations that *are* oppressive organizations. There is imperfection on both sides.

In the 1994 *Nahrstedt* decision the California Supreme Court pointed out that there is a third party to these battles over some seemingly trivial issues—the other homeowners who rely on the CC&Rs being upheld. These *forgotten people* are the ones who want nothing more than to live in a well-regulated community.

Owners may have purchased their units **because** of certain restrictions. Someone allergic to cats bought into a "no-pets" condominium for a good reason. Shouldn't they be able to rely on no pets being allowed? The manager and directors must address these issues and call violations to the attention of owners.

Many of these cases are reported in a simplified way by the press. Emotions rather than facts dominate the stories. One sure-fire way to make an association, or any other authority, look evil is to involve the American flag.

A tire shop flies thirty U.S. flags in violation of federal and local codes and alleges freedom of speech and patriotism as its motive rather than advertising.

A high school student challenges his school's dress code by wearing a tee shirt with an American flag on it.

The directors are obligated to uphold the CC&Rs or they could face personal liability. Since few people who have volunteered for an uncompensated job overseeing a multimillion dollar property want to be sued for their efforts, they try to enforce the rules. They are still vilified in the press more often than not. It has become so predictable as to be cliché. And I'm so very tired.

Q: *I called the manager on his emergency line and got charged. What's the deal?*

CONDOGURU: The problem seems to be with the definition of *emergency.* I checked into your call and learned that your concern was with your neighbor's cat using your lawn for a powder room at 11:22 PM Saturday night.

I can see how that might qualify as an emergency should the next door cat be a Bengal tiger, but there is no evidence that is the case.

Since the association has to pay management for after-hour calls and special trips, the cost of a frivolous call is passed on to you, Bwana.

An emergency is loosely defined as fire, insurrection and flood. For the fire call 9-1-1. For the insurrection call the Marines. Flooding or other property damage is a job for management. The manager is not competing with the police, fire department or paramedics. Consider the severity of the situation and who can best help before calling—you will get the right kind of help sooner and the manager will get some sleep, bless his heart.

Q: *I wanted a list of names and addresses of members of my association so I could send out some advertising for my business. The manager won't give them to me. He's obstructing free trade.*

CONDOGURU: Since your association is a corporation and has to function under the California *Corporations Code* (and a bunch of other statutes), the manager was only following the law. As a member, you have a right to membership lists but only **for purposes reasonably related to your interest as a member.** An example would be if you were running for the board or organizing a recall election. Membership lists can't be provided for commercial purposes (unless you cut me in for a percentage).

Q: *I was looking at a copy of the minutes from a board meeting that was posted on the bulletin board. It barely covered a single page. Aren't the minutes supposed to detail what went on at the meeting? I belong to a stamp-collecting club with longer minutes.*

CONDOGURU: Since your association is a not-for-profit corporation, state law governs the keeping of meeting minutes. The minutes or a summary have to be made available, even if in draft form, to the membership within 30 days of the meeting date. They don't have to be distributed, only made available to the members.

There isn't any requirement to record board deliberations, only what was decided, that's why they are so slim.

"I'm not crazy about this new batch of directors."

"How come?"

"He thinks they are too rigid."

"Isn't that why they're called a "board?'"

CHAPTER 11

The Role of Volunteers

Who, me?

The top ten excuses for not serving on the board:

- *I don't have the time.*
- *The others are doing a fine job.*
- *I don't like making decisions.*
- *I don't have the time.*
- *I moved here so someone else would take care of things.*
- *No one likes the board members.*
- *It's a lot of work without compensation.*
- *That's what we have a manager for.*
- *I don't want to be sued.*
- *I don't have the time.*

Whether it's little league practice, cub scouts, a second job, travel, or a full dance card, very few people have (or are willing to take) time to serve on their homeowner association board. Those who have (or would find) the time are often concerned about potential legal liability. It's no secret that California is a litigious society—and community associations have not been spared. Those who have served know that it can be a thankless job carrying a ton of responsibility with no monetary compensation.

Board members are essential to a community association. Even with the presence of an experienced, professional CID property manager, it is still up to the board to set policies, make decisions, and watch over the interests of all the residents. The role of director is important and demanding. It is a wise community that gives recognition and applauds the people willing to serve.

Besides directors, other volunteers are necessary to a smooth running community. If the board is left without help to meet all the association's leadership, management and legal obligations—not to mention the niceties such as social functions—directors can burn out. When no one steps forward to assume responsibility the association faces a serious problem.

Carefree Living—An Incentive To Buy

Condominium property is often sold with the promise that it is the perfect investment because *other people* take care of your property for you. The *no sweat* investment sales pitch can be misleading, but once escrow closes the realtor may not be particularly concerned with who does the sweating. Buyers are led away from the idea that some additional commitment might be expected.

There is no legal liability for an individual refusing to serve on a board, but there are significant ramifications for all owners if *no one* is willing to serve—and this worst-possible situation can and does occur. When it happens, the association can get into big trouble. If no one fills out necessary corporate papers each year and the corporation loses its status, it loses its authority to act. If there is no one to collect money and pay the bills, no maintenance gets done. If no one is there to take control, the CC&Rs won't be enforced. When a CID is missing a board of directors, it will soon miss many other services. The courts may step in with a remedy in the form of a court-appointed receiver to run things—and that person will be compensated from association funds. The association without competent board leadership is a rudderless ship, not a place where anyone would want to live for long—or buy into.

How do CID members overcome their reluctance to serve? Mostly through education and recognition of the vital nature of the job. What follows are answers to some common questions potential volunteers ask.

Q: *Aren't boards usually retired people?*

A: Board members include business owners, teachers, salespersons, executives, managers, government workers, retail clerks, homemakers, engineers, professionals *and* retired people—a cross-section of the community. Directors serve for various reasons. Most are people who care about operation of the association and how their money is spent. Some simply agree to run because there are not enough nominees to meet vacancies. Some like the idea of being in control. There is prestige in the position. Directors may be proactive—leaders, followers or supporters.

Q: *I just rent here. Don't you have to be an owner?*

A: Some associations' bylaws make provisions for non-owners to serve on the board. Sometimes they can serve as voting board members, and sometimes they are limited to advisory positions. In communities with a high percentage of non-owner tenants or lessees, residents should become familiar with how board decisions affect them. Non-owners may not be actively recruited as volunteers, even where the right to serve exists. Even when no formal positions are available for tenants, a wise board would encourage tenant participation on committees and in other activities. Successful CIDs address the interests of resident owners, nonresident owners, and their tenants. Chapter 12 addresses this subject in detail.

Q: *I don't live here. I own a unit and rent it out. Can I serve?*

A: Nonresident owners can, and should, serve on the board unless the CC&Rs don't allow it. Everyone should know what's going on with their investment and all perspectives should be represented in some capacity on the board or in committees. What directors do directly affects property values and the CID's desirability in the rental market. The resident owners, on whose shoulders board responsibilities usually fall, may come to resent watching over property that is an income source for someone who they never see.

HOW A VOLUNTEER ASKS, "HOW CAN I HELP?"

"Why doesn't <u>somebody</u> do <u>something</u> around here?

Q: *I would like to be on the board but I don't know anything about what directors do. I'm really bad at business, flunked typing in high school. Would the board want me?*

A: Directors have a primary goal—to protect, maintain and enhance the value of the property, and a secondary goal of preserving "quiet enjoyment of the property" for the residents. A desire to serve the community is an admirable reason to volunteer. Some people obviously have more education or expertise than others. Depending on how many stand for election, there might be positions for everyone who is willing. If there is competition, then candidates may be chosen because of a greater reliance on their professional qualifications. If there is insufficient expertise among directors to make informed decisions, boards may engage a property manager to oversee operation of the community and advise the volunteers. For tough decisions, the board has a right to consult with professionals—lawyers, accountants, architects, etc.—at the expense of the association, and to rely on that advice. Directors are generally protected from lawsuits relating to their duties and decisions unless they can be proven capricious or malicious, or they are acting outside their capacity as a board member. Their decisions don't have to be right—just arrived at reasonably.

The only qualifications for directors are the desire to serve the community, to protect their investments, and the resolve to not always leave it up to others. The job becomes an education in itself and there are many opportunities to learn. Plus, it couldn't hurt your résumé to list "director of a multimillion dollar corporation."

Without Volunteers—There is No Community

In many communities, there is a noticeable and definite shortage of volunteers. CIDs are a unique form of living, as any resident of a condo or planned unit development will attest. Typically, CIDs are nonprofit, mutual benefit corporations subject to the California *Corporations Code*. It is interesting to note that even unincorporated CIDs gain some corporate attributes under *The Davis-Stirling Act*.

What makes CIDs unique is that the corporation has such an all-encompassing effect on the lives of its members—the same volunteer members who become the corporate officers drive the operation. These volunteers carry a lot of responsibility without compensation other than the appreciation of some of their neighbors or having a say in decisions affecting their property. A CID is, in many ways, a microcosm of city government (as described in previous chapters). Large CIDs may have populations in the tens of thousands and multimillion dollar operating budgets. Others might have fewer than ten units and minuscule budgets. Yet, from the largest to the smallest, they are all treated essentially the same under California law.

Both large and small CIDs operate with elected boards of directors. These community leaders tackle many of the challenges that directors of a *Fortune 500* corporation might face. They must devise budgets and manage assets and predict future reserve fund requirements: when streets will need sealcoating, roofs replacing, or the recreational facilities upgrading.

CIDs with more than a few units often hire a management service, whether it be simply to keep the books and handle finances, or to provide complete oversight of the property. Regardless of the CID's size, its type of management or total value, it needs leadership that must be provided by volunteers.

CIDs need more than just directors to function. Volunteers of every stripe will make a difference, whether organizing a block party, welcoming new residents, or providing expertise for developing a service contract. Committees might be appointed to review architectural or landscaping change requests, or to follow changes in the law or track down educational materials. They might be appointed to serve as community liaisons, as an ombudsman to coordinate resident and owner information and assistance, or to analyze the impact of government decisions on their communities.

Neighbors Helping Neighbors

In some associations organizing the community to fight crime is an especially important function. Crime prevention programs have various names but Neighborhood Watch and Crime Stoppers are two of the better known. The name is much less im-

EFFECTIVE MOB CONTROL TECHNIQUE

One step closer and you'll all be declared
candidates for the board of directors.

portant than the will of community volunteers to embrace a crime
prevention plan.

In some of the worst areas there has been a recent trend toward voluntary citizen patrols to "take back the streets" from the
criminals, the punks, the graffiti vandals, the drug dealers. These
patrols have come about because of an increasing awareness by
residents that their neighborhood is heading in the wrong direction
and police alone can't do the job.

For those fainter of heart but with a will to serve, there are ways to help their community—enhancing community spirit or acting as staff to help directors meet their obligations. Some communities use selection committees to find and interview professionals and service providers such as landscapers and contractors. Some have enforcement committees to hear matters related to CC&R or rule violations. There are budgetary or financial committees to sort out money matters. Associations even have social committees.

What are some CID volunteer problems?

Apathy

Apathy is probably the *number one* problem in CIDs—people who don't care, who don't want to get involved, and those who simply don't pay attention to their community until there is a crisis. It isn't uncommon, for the sake of a sale, that owners are led to believe someone else has complete responsibility for their property. They may not even *know* that they can volunteer to serve. Those who buy condos often have busy lives—that's why they buy in a place where the lawns get mowed, the pool gets cleaned and the trees get trimmed "automatically". They may be too busy to read newsletters or ballot measures, let alone commit to volunteer service that would further cut into their time. A leaky roof, a large special assessment, a recall meeting or an earthquake may be necessary to attract their attention.

Liability and Insurance

Legal liability is an ever-present concern. The more we participate in society, the greater the chance for some kind of liability. Serving on boards and committees does expose one to some liability. It's extremely important for CIDs to ensure that sufficient insurance protection is in place for board *and* committee members. Although there is higher exposure for the board since it is the ultimate decision-maker and authority, residents will be more willing to serve on committees if they know they are also protected. Coverage should also be extended to liaisons who are appointed as a committee of one. A board should have specific procedures for appointing committees so there is no question of a person's status within the corporation. The directors and officers (D&O) errors and omissions insurance should be checked to make sure designated committee members are covered.

Limitations on Authority

When volunteers are appointed for committees or tasks, they need to clearly understand their roles. Most often, volunteers make recommendations to the board who will then decide what action to take. Volunteers unsure of their authority limits may commit the association to an action it would not otherwise choose to take. A committee member who oversteps his or her authority may create problems—especially if association members, in good faith, rely on the volunteer's imagined or asserted authority.

CONDOGURU SPEAKS

Q: *I'm thinking about running for the board of directors next year, but I'm not sure what they do or how much they get paid.*

CONDOGURU: Some folks hold that directors get paid what they are worth. Nothing. Of course those are often the same folks who believe that directors are really politicians.

The reality is that directors serve as volunteers. According to California *Corporations Code*, section 7231.5(b), a "volunteer" is someone who renders services without compensation. As a practical matter, the association has to have some way to make decisions for all the members. That's the role of the board of directors. There is a clear distinction between directors and management—management gets paid, but the directors get to boss him or her around. Actually, the relationship between manager and the board of directors is, ideally, a partnership. Directors make decisions and spend association funds often relying on the expertise of the manager for guidance.

Directors are your neighbors who have accepted responsibility for the operation of the complex. Their duties are many but their mandate, their reason for being, is simply to *protect the value of the property*. Those are only a few words, but they are far-reaching in their implication.

Protecting the value of the commonly-held property involves maintenance of the physical plant such as buildings, recreational facilities, some utilities, landscaping and streets. But there is more to protecting property value than simply maintaining the grounds. There are subtler effects that can drive down the perceived value of the property. For example, if the property is located in a high crime area, its value could be depressed. Obviously, directors can't move the property to a better area but they can form a Neighborhood Watch, hire a security patrol, and keep residents informed and aware of the problems.

At times when all property values are dropping, little can be done to keep real estate prices up. Directors face the task of maintaining *relative* value in the market.

This may sound as though directors spend their time making real estate decisions. That isn't the case. The best way to hold or even enhance market value is to simply carry out a program that any well-run corporation would to maintain the assets, invest wisely, hire the best help, and give each action careful consideration. It is what any prudent businessperson would do. That is the standard that directors must try to maintain. This is the *business judgment rule* that must be observed in their decisions.

Any homeowner in good standing is eligible to serve on the board. Attend a few meetings, get to know the directors, serve on a committee or two. It is *your* property at stake.

Q: *I have noticed that the market price for my unit has gone down since I bought it. I thought the directors were supposed to protect my property values—since you're on the subject.*

CONDOGURU: Surely you're jesting. Yes, the directors' stated goal is to maintain property values but they don't control or influence the real estate market. It doesn't look like anyone does. The best your directors can do is maintain the value of the property *relative* to the market.

Is there any liability for them if the market value of your unit declines *relative* to the market? It would be an uphill battle to make such a case if you could even find a lawyer to take it.

You would have to prove that one or more directors acted in bad faith or were grossly negligent. *Civil Code* §1365.7 specifically limits director liability. Something else to keep in mind, the directors are unpaid volunteers who are owners of units. Wouldn't you think they would have a personal interest in keeping up the value of the property. If you have ideas how they can do a better job, I know they would welcome your participation.

Now, about the condition of your unit....

Q: *We don't like what the board is doing. Can we get up a petition to fire them?*

El Cid

I'll take this one Guru, because it keeps coming up and it's a sticky legal problem. My initial thought is: How can you fire somebody who doesn't get paid?

Actually, when owners are unhappy and want to get rid of a board member or the entire board, they have to go through a process to *un*elect them—much like the government's impeachment or recall of a politician. There must be an *election* to unseat them. In certain extreme cases, such as fraud or criminal activity, or loss of ability to serve (mental illness or incapacity), directors can be unseated by court order. But they can't just be "fired" or unseated by signatures on a petition.

PART 4

FOR NON-OWNERS AND NONRESIDENT OWNERS

CHAPTER 12   RENTING A CONDOMINIUM

CHAPTER 12

Renting a Condominium

Renter: *I just rent my place. I didn't sign any agreement with the association so you can take your CC&Rs and rules and shove 'em.*

Investor-owner: *I just rent my place out. Why don't you bug my tenant instead of me if you don't like what he's doing? Why does the association have a manager if he isn't going to manage?*

Board Member/Manager: *He's a renter—that's the problem. He doesn't care about the condo or the neighbors. You know about those renters—just trouble.*

These comments reflect three common perspectives on rentals in condo developments or planned unit developments, tightly-held prejudices that are often the basis of deeply divisive rifts in the community. In this chapter we explore the roots of these views, their effect on the association, and some ways in which these competing interests can be brought to a common focus. We examine how one association has turned the difficult circumstance brought about by a large number of rentals into an association asset.

Homeownership is the keystone of the American dream. We hear it from childhood on—the little white cottage with a picket fence and a thirty-year mortgage—a cliché in itself, illuminated by still more clichés: Home is where the heart is; where you hang your hat; where, when you go there they have to take you in.

> *Home, the spot of earth supremely blest,*
> *A dearer, sweeter spot than all the rest.*
>   —Robert Montgomery

> *Until the rent goes up.*
>   —Condoguru

The Renter's Perspective

"We're just renters." What does it mean? It could be: *Since we don't own here, we don't have to follow the rules.* How about: *We live here—but we don't have any rights even though we're just as good as anybody else.*

Perhaps the clearest distinction of economic class in our society, whether true or perceived, is the difference between owners and renters. *Renter*, to some, is a term of derision which leads seamlessly into the *them and us* mindset that permeates many discussions of the subject.

Why Rent?

The desire for mobility and affordability brings many who have no intention of owning a home flocking to condos and PUDs. Many possess the wherewithal to purchase but aren't interested. They are attracted by amenities that come without an "apartment atmosphere." The design of many condo complexes gives the sense of privacy and luxury one would expect in a house but without the yard work of a single home rental. That's attractive to many in our mobile society who have not been mesmerized by the "picket fence" dream and who place a priority on maximizing their leisure time.

*In our mobile society many people like the
ability to move at will that renting affords them.*

Then there are those who covet ownership of a condo castle and are working toward that achievement while in the meantime living a version of their dream in a rented condo.

There may be any number of reasons why the rental population in common interest developments is increasing, including fluctuating property values in the rental market since the 1970's and local vacancy rates. Negative pressures on the California real estate market reflect military base closures, corporate flight from state over-regulation and the high cost of doing business.

Many homeowners have been left holding a mortgage that exceeds the value of the property. These owners feel stuck, knowing that a sale, or an attempt to sell, could have serious financial consequences. Mortgage money has tightened up in the condo market and tight money makes it difficult to move up from a condominium by trading. Condo owners find they may be able to afford a single home not by selling their condo in a depressed market, but by renting it out. Increased rental availability reduces rent prices and condominiums are generally more attractive than apartments. The result is that in many CIDs the balance of owner-occupied and tenant-occupied units tips toward rentals.

Still, a perception persists that renters, who are necessary to this equation, are of somehow lower quality than property owners. The amusing paradox is that most owners were themselves, at one time, renters in search of a thirty-year mortgage. It may simply be inconvenient for them to remember.

There are bad renters just as there are bad owners—ask any property manager responsible for a CID. But there is no reason to consider "just renters" bad neighbors unless they have risen to the challenge and earned the title.

A Resident Owner's Perspective

"The place is crawlin' with renters. I can't get refinanced because of 'em and I can't sell because nobody will finance anybody wanting to buy into a place with so many renters."

Whose fault is it that properties with a high percentage of rentals are difficult to sell or refinance? The 1986 Barton-Silverman Department of Real Estate Study indicates a higher likelihood of problems in a development with a large number of rental units. Word-of-mouth recountings of difficult experiences with *government-subsidized* housing tenants and the responsible *government entity*—such as its failure to assist with tenants' problems—have fueled debate on the issue of renters in CIDs. Secondary mortgage market lenders have imposed lending restrictions on developments with a high percentage of rentals. Legal reserve requirements enacted in recent years have caused increased lender scrutiny of an association's financial status. The resentment of the industry and those who have experienced difficulties in obtaining financing—and who often take the problem to the board of directors—has created an anti-renter backlash that *ignores the individual and vilifies the entire class.*

But rentals are inevitable. So the question is what to do about them—treat renters like lepers or amend the governing documents to ban them from the community?

Treating renters as diseased will not resolve the problem. Rather, it will increase tensions. Renters, whatever else they may be, are human and deserve dignified treatment. Intentionally creating a two-class society is antithetical to the entire concept of *community* and cooperative living. Aside from anger and resentment, what can be achieved by creating an outsider faction? There is no way it could it possibly help preserve property values.

KEY POINT
Renters *treated* as outsiders may be forgiven for *acting* like outsiders; if treated as neighbors, then there is a good chance they will become neighbors in the best sense of the word.

Amending the CC&Rs to prohibit or limit leasing is somewhat controversial in this state and not a move to be made without good legal advice. When making a lease-limiting restriction is contemplated in a CID where a high number of rentals is perceived as a problem, it may prove very difficult to achieve the required number of votes necessary to amend the CC&Rs. Unless there is a generous "grandfather" clause allowing current leases to continue in spite of the limitation, the board would be asking the rental unit owners to vote *against* their own financial interests. These rental owners are often the same people who have moved to single family homes and are now facing two mortgage payments. They may depend on rental income and without it could face bankruptcy.

Rentals are a fact of life. Whether leased condominium units are a problem for resident owners or not, responsibility for creating the rental is that of its owner, not the family who answered the ad for, "Clean, quiet condo, park-like setting, amenities."

KEY POINT

Rentals are created by *owners* of the condominium units. The inhabitants merely responded to an opportunity to live in a pleasant community. The nonresident owners bear responsibility for problem renters.

The Investor-Owner Perspective

Investor-owners fall into two categories: those who have once lived in their unit and those who have not. There is likely to be a difference in the attitude each has toward the property. The exresident-investor-owner who bought the property as a starter home has an emotional as well as an economic attachment to the place. It once was home, where children were brought up, where memories of happy and sorrowful events reside. The interest they have in the property is born of intimate knowledge and a connection to friends who still live there. Bonds to the old community may dissolve over time, but the outlook is different than that of the investor who has never lived in the home.

The unconnected investor-owner seldom feels a tie to the community and interest is likely to be purely financial. These emotionally-detached owners have little impetus to become concerned with the community until their tenant becomes the association's pain in the neck and the owner is threatened with legal action or fines because of tenant conduct.

The Board of Directors' Perspective

Each of the "players" we have seen so far—the tenant, the resident owner, the nonresident investor-owner—are single-minded entities. Not so the board of directors. The association comprises all owners with the board of directors at the nucleus. Directors are charged with operating the association for the benefit of all the owners, regardless of where they live. The board members may come from any of the owner groups depending upon what association bylaws allow.

Within the parameters of the bylaws, board composition depends primarily on the groups and individuals who are most interested in what is going on. In a development that is heavily rentals, the investors may be more likely to serve on the board because of a shortage of resident owners. Their investments are at stake. Some feel that a board made up of investors is more likely to function in accordance with law, in a more business-like manner, and be demanding of good management practices—consistent with a purely financial attachment to the CID. Others feel that resident owners should be making the decisions that directly affect their current home and primary investment.

Nonresident owners may be less likely to work with residents' best interests in mind and vice versa. Investor owners may opt for reduced maintenance or oppose special assessments in the interest of keeping their cost of doing business low as possible. Resident owner directors may opt to improve the facilities so residents derive greater enjoyment out of the property.

Commonly, there is a larger pool of interested resident owners than nonresident owners and that is reflected in the board's makeup. Investors may resist involvement with the board of directors as long as they feel the association board is adequately protecting their property. Indeed, why would an investor spend time working on a community board when there is no additional tangible benefit, when to do so would not add a penny to income from the rental but would use valuable time?

Facts and Friction

Let's take the story of Nirvana Homeowner Association as an example of how the tables can be turned around to utilize and include renters as a resource. Of Nirvana's 200 units, half are rental properties. The nonresident owners do not involve themselves in the association's operation and are heard from only when there is a problem that will cost them money. Occasionally the Nirvana manager or board president will receive a call from one of the nonresident owners asking for some favor, such as to check on a tenant whose rent payment is late and whose phone has been disconnected.

After making a few calls for absent owners and dealing with other renter-inspired events, the president and other board members began to resent the long-distance association members.

If there weren't any renters, they reasoned, the association would have to print and mail only 200 newsletters, not 300. When reroofing and termite eradication projects were done, the coordinators had to deal not only with owners (by long distance), but with renters too—fifty percent extra hassle. The moving vans were at the complex every week. With so many renters the turnover was so fast that diesel rigs seemed to block the streets daily and the association welcome wagon volunteer was run ragged and threatened to quit.

Association costs would be lower if the hundred rentals were owner occupied. Since mass evictions and forced return of the owners were impossible, an idea circulated among the directors that the nonresident owners ought to bear a larger share of the association's costs related to rental properties. It is because of them that money has to be spent on an extra hundred of almost everything—extra rule books, extra notices. And all the work falls on the shoulders of the residents who do all the volunteering, stamp licking, everything. The nonresident owners just show up at the annual meeting and complain the board and manager aren't responsive to their demands. None of them are willing to serve on the board or even write an article for the newsletter. And when they get a new tenant they don't even notify the manager or call the welcoming committee. The manager or board has to figure out who has arrived by the moving van tracks in the new asphalt sealcoat.

This resentment of the nonresident owners tainted the way the *renters* were regarded. The renters had become a daily, visible reminder of what had become for the Nirvana directors an ongoing, nagging, seemingly unresolvable situation.

But to blame the renters was to be illogical, short-sighted, petty and would ultimately pit neighbor against neighbor. To their credit, the Nirvana directors saw community stratification as an even bigger negative than rental units.

A Solution is Found

When Nirvana directors finally decided to examine their situation objectively, they found that the resident owners and tenants had many common concerns. All cared about safety and security and the attractiveness of the grounds. Renters were just as irritated about moving vans blocking their driveways and kids riding bicycles on the landscaping as owners were. They were just as annoyed by loud stereos and the incessant noise of skateboards on the sidewalks. Nirvana renters thought of themselves as having a financial stake in the complex—they paid every month to live there. They wanted the best living conditions possible for the money they sent to the landlord.

Some tenants had purchased units in the complex after living there and could be credited with beginning a trend toward reversal of the ratio of renters to owners.

Nirvana's president proposed a bold move: Change the by-laws to add two appointed advisory director positions to the board to be filled by renters. They wouldn't be voting positions since it would be inappropriate for non-owners to vote on measures to spend money that wasn't theirs, but the new directors would join debates and give a voice to fifty percent of the residents.

The message: Renters were now officially considered *part of the community* and were regarded as *contributing members*.

In a program to expand on the concept, renters were actively recruited for committees and the Neighborhood Watch. Their contributions to the community were recognized at annual meetings with awards and in the newsletter. The pejorative term "renter" was abandoned for "neighbor" or "resident." The fact of ownership became the footnote rather than the headline.

The pool of volunteers that had dwindled through the absence of nonresident owners was replenished by inviting the tenants to join in and serve their community. All the residents had reason to protect the property because whether they owned it or not, *it was their home.* And when it came time to buy, Nirvana became a more attractive prospect for those in the market, further improving the owner-renter ratio.

There were still those owners who refused to get past their notion of "us verses them" but less was heard from that quarter when "them" became valued, contributing members of the Nirvana community.

The Nirvana board took an enlightened approach and invited renters to participate in the community. Not all boards can be counted on to be so welcoming or engaging. Nevertheless, renters can make the first move. Few boards would turn down an enthusiastic volunteer who offered to monitor the pool two hours a day, or help on the summer picnic committee, or organize a block party or serve as Neighborhood Watch coordinator.

Problems abound, multiplying when no one takes a positive step toward solving them. Renters, residents, investors, the board of directors—anyone can make the difference by making the effort. In our imperfect society there will always be those who are ready to assess blame. Those who want to make a difference do not need an organization, only a desire and the gumption to make it happen.

Condoguru Speaks

Q: *I rent my unit from the owner who lives in Alaska. He doesn't seem to care about fixing anything, and the association manager is no better. He never responds to my calls.*

CONDOGURU: This is a commonly misunderstood area. The association (and the manager) have no legal relationship with anyone other than the unit owner. Unlike an *apartment* manager, the *association* manager has no authority or control over routine matters in your unit. That is exclusively between you and Nanook of the North. You might suggest to him (Nanook) that he appoint a local agent for his property. That is in both your and his best interest and it gives the association a local contact.

Thanks for the information on Nanook. I hear your association has been wondering where he had gone.

Q: *Why should I give a hoot about CC&Rs? I rent here and I didn't sign any promise to abide by them.*

CONDOGURU: True enough; you didn't sign but your unit owner did. The essence of condominium life is that all the owners share equally in the obligations and derive equal misery. Some owners choose to rent out their property. That does not change their obligation to the association, though it could increase their misery.

The association retains a legal relationship with the owner but not the tenant. This leads to the management and directors referring to the unit itself as the *entity* with which it has the contract. It isn't *you* who left your garbage can out an hour too long, it is unit 42's garbage can. The violation notice goes to unit 42's owner. To the association, a renter is the same as a guest of the owner. The owner is responsible for the unit's (your) actions.

Let's say for the sake of illustration that your kids chop down a 40-foot eucalyptus in the common area. A bill for the cost of replacing the tree goes to your unit owner. He has some choices. He can elect not to pay the bill and end up in court; he can pay the bill and reduce the value of your Christmas present by a like amount; he can pay the bill and ask you to pay him back; or he could ask you to vacate the unit and still pay the bill.

He pays the bill in any case. Your popularity with him is likely to diminish as a result. The association encourages you to be a good neighbor by hammering unit 42's owner who gets to hammer you. Think of yourself as a hammeree-once-removed.

Q: *After I moved in to my rental unit some people from the association came by and wanted me to sign a compliance form. What is it?*

CONDOGURU: Some associations use these forms to get a commitment from renters to follow the rules. In my opinion the compliance form is a waste of time. The association already has a way to make you comply through the owner's obligation. (see the preceding question). I would rather see an association simply <u>welcome</u> the new resident rather than come on like a parent on prom night. The welcome committee should be able to supply you with a rule book if the owner didn't.

The association does not have a legal relationship with renters and a compliance form doesn't establish one. The owner is still responsible.

Q: *Do I need insurance as a renter?*

CONDOGURU: Yes! Just because you live in a rental unit, don't assume that your landlady's insurance covers your liabilities. Why should it? She is interested in protecting her buns *from* you.

There are standard renters insurance policies that will cover your personal property and liability. Many individual policies include accidental damage coverage (when you flood your unit or break someone else's property even while away from your residence). Some will cover intentional damage by children under 13 years—like that 40-foot eucalyptus tree they cut down.

AFTERWORD

*Backward Harry brushed the goat chow off
his blazer and said, "Mr. President..."*

BACKWARD HARRY
TURNS THINGS AROUND

We left Backward Harry at the Fracas Falls annual homeowners meeting with a face full of goat chow and the angry hoots of his fellow association members ringing in his ears. Harry was undeterred by the derision heaped on him by the others. He stood his ground because he was dedicated to the moral principles his mother taught him when he was just a backward baby.

Harry took a moment to brush the goat chow from his handsomely checkered blazer and waited for the room to quiet. "Mr. President," he said in his respectful way, "I believe I can help the good citizens of Fracas Falls HOA turn things around. We have reached a critical point and if we fail to return to and embrace the concept of cooperative living, I fear that Fracas Falls will become an environment of constant battling that may land us in court and cost us all more than we can afford—not to mention the emotional strain." Harry's left foot began a time step again as he warmed to the subject and the audience reluctantly turned eyes toward him.

"I withdraw my offer to serve on the Means and Ways Committee," he said. "Instead, I am announcing my write-in candidacy for the board and I challenge Mr. Goat Farmer, Mr. Yugo Collector and Mr. Balcony Spa to join me."

The big talkers were trapped. Saving face would mean offering themselves up for election just to keep an eye on Harry. And each knew, deep in his soul that the goats would have to go, the Yugos would have to go, and the spa couldn't perch on the balcony. To allow such violations, as directors, would be hypocritical and the only thing they feared more than Backward Harry as a director with authority over them was being called hypocrites.

Mr. Goat Farmer, who was already thinking about finding a good home for his goats, Boo Boo, Dockers and Tulip, was the first to speak. "Mr. President, I offer my name as a write-in candidate for director." He sat down heavily, thinking about changes he'd have to make in his own life in order to serve as an example for others while he absently chewed a chunk of goat chow.

"Me too," said Mr. Yugo Collector, not to be outdone by Mr. Goat Farmer who he feared would get soft on Backward Harry and gang up on him about the Yugos.

"Count me in," said Mr. Balcony Spa, who didn't trust anyone.

They didn't all live in perfect happiness ever after because life is never perfect. There were further fracases, notably with Mr. Chickens in the Garage, Mrs. Clean White Wash Hanging On A Line, and The Fracas Falls HOA Skateboard and Garage Sale Club, but between the new and old board members and an emerging attitude of cautious cooperation, things began to change for the better. Fracas Falls became a nicer place to live—and that's life as it ought to be.

GLOSSARY OF TERMS
AS USED IN THIS BOOK

Articles of Incorporation: A charter document filed with the state that creates corporate status for a common interest development.

Association: A nonprofit corporation or homeowner group that is unincorporated, created for the purpose of managing a common interest development.

Board of Directors: The elected, deliberative body responsible for managing, planning, setting policy and operation of a homeowner association/common interest development.

Bylaws: An organizational document that sets up the structure and guides the board of directors in operating the corporation.

CC&Rs: Covenants, Conditions and Restrictions (sometimes called the "declaration"). A document that describes restrictions on the way land may be used. The key governing document for common interest developments.

CID: Common Interest Development. A community apartment project, condominium project, a planned development or stock cooperative.

Common Area: The entire CID except for separate interests.

Common Interest Development: (see CID)

Community Apartment Project: A CID in which an undivided interest in land is coupled with the right of exclusive occupancy of any apartment located thereon.

Condominium: An undivided interest in a common area with the other owners coupled with a separate interest in a space called a unit.

Condominium Plan: A plan that describes the physical characteristics of a condominium project.

Condominium Project: A development consisting of condominiums.

Declarant: The person or group that signs the original declaration of CC&Rs establishing a common interest development, often the developer of the CID.

Declaration: (see CC&Rs)

Director: A member of the board of directors. In most cases a director is an uncompensated homeowner volunteer who is elected by vote of the association membership.

Exclusive Use Common Area: A portion of the common area that is designated for the exclusive use of one or more, but fewer than all of the owners of separate interests. May be designated in the CC&Rs. Certain exclusive use common areas are identified by law.

Fiduciary Duty: Literally, a duty of trust depending on public confidence. Practically, it is the duty (of a director) to consider the best interests of the entire association when making corporate decisions. The duty includes an obligation to put self interest aside if it conflicts with the best interests of the association.

Governing Documents: The declaration of CC&Rs and other documents such as bylaws, articles of incorporation and rules which govern operation of the association.

Homeowner Association (HOA): The collective group of home-owners in a common interest development.

Member: A person or persons entitled to membership in the association, usually by virtue of ownership of a separate interest.

Nonseverability: Usually a "severance" clause in the CC&Rs of a CID that prevents a member from separating his or her interest in the common area from that of the rest of the membership.

Owner: The record owner of a separate interest. A "member" of the association by virtue of ownership in a separate interest.

Planned [Unit] Development (PUD): A PUD is generally a CID with common area, usually owned by the association. Separate "lots" are owned by individual members.

Pro forma: An item or document provided in advance in a pre-scribed form. The association must provide a "pro forma" budget to the membership each year in advance of the start of the fiscal year

PUD: (see Planned [Unit] Development)

Restricted Common Areas: Same as Exclusive Use Common Area. When Restricted Common Areas exist, they are usually designated on the condominium plan.

Rules/Regulations: The association document, which is normally prepared at the direction of the board of directors, that serves as a common reference for members of the CID and reflects CC&Rs and official policy. Sometimes owners are allowed to vote on adoption of rules and/or regulations.

Separate Interest: In a *community apartment project*, the exclusive right to occupy an apartment; in a *condominium project*, an individual unit (the interior airspace); in a *planned [unit] development*, a separately owned lot, parcel, area, or space; in a *stock co-operative*, the exclusive right to occupy a portion of the real property.

Stock Cooperative: A CID in which a corporation is formed to hold title in a property and the corporation is owned by shareholders who have a right to occupy a portion of the real property.

Tenants in Common: Partners in ownership of property.

Townhouse: A style of housing structure that employs common walls.

Unit: The separate interest in a condominium project. This is the residential, exclusive use area often referred to as the "air space" within the building that is owned by the individual member.

APPENDIX

COMMON INTEREST DEVELOPMENT
INDUSTRY ORGANIZATIONS

California Association of Community Managers (CACM)
18662 MacArthur Blvd., Suite 340
Irvine, CA 92715
(714) 263-CACM
FAX (714) 263-3789

Club Lake Association of Northern California (CLANC)
c/o Bill Stewart
11509 Northwoods Blvd.
Truckee, CA 96161
(916) 587-9494
FAX (916) 587-9419

Community Associations Institute (CAI)—National Office
1630 Duke St.
Alexandria, VA 22314
(703) 548-8600
FAX (703) 684-1581

CAI CALIFORNIA CHAPTERS

CAI San Francisco Bay Area Chapter
1989A Santa Rita Rd., Suite 260
Pleasanton, CA 94566
(510) 803-0860
FAX (510) 803-0861

CAI California North Chapter
2848 Arden Way, Suite 200
Sacramento, CA 95825
(916) 974-8390
FAX (916) 974-8380

CAI Central California Chapter
P.O. Box 70262
Stockton, CA 95267
(209) 477-7314
FAX (209) 474-2406

CAI Mid California Chapter
c/o CAFS, Inc.
218 W. Carmen Lane, #111
Santa Maria, CA 93454
(805) 928-1980
FAX (805) 922-5360

CAI Channel Islands Chapter
P.O. Box 3795
Ventura, CA 93006
(805) 658-1438
FAX (805) 658-1732

CAI Coachella Valley Chapter
41-865 Boardwalk, Suite 121
Palm Desert, CA 92211
(619) 341-0559
FAX (619) 341-8843

CAI Greater Inland Empire Chapter
P.O. Box 8478
Moreno Valley, CA 92552
(909) 653-5893
FAX (909) 653-2283

CAI Greater Los Angeles Chapter
P.O. Box 84303
Los Angeles, CA 90073
(310) 285-8286
FAX (310) 576-0485

CAI Orange County Regional Chapter
23421 South Pointe Dr., Suite 145
Laguna Hills, CA 92653
(714) 380-7360
FAX (714) 380-4312

CAI San Diego Chapter
P.O. Box 420730
San Diego, CA 92142
(619) 467-1224
(FAX (619) 467-1704

**Council of Condominium Homeowners Associations, Inc.
(COCHA)**
P.O. Box 4484
Walnut Creek, CA 94596-4484
(510) 937-0177

Executive Council of Homeowners (ECHO)
1602 The Alameda, Suite 100
San Jose, CA 95126-2308
(408) 297-3246
FAX (408) 297-3517

Sacramento Area Condominium Association (SACA)
P.O. Box 160246
Sacramento, CA 95816
(916) 923-2203

ABOUT THE AUTHORS

Beth A. Grimm
Attorney at Law

Beth A. Grimm is a recognized authority on community association law who calls upon many years experience dealing with the problems of homeowners and their associations. An accomplished writer, she publishes the *California Homeowners Association Legal Digest* and contributes to and serves as legislative editor of *Community Living in California*, a newsletter for community associations.

As a volunteer speaker and writer for community association industry groups she is heavily involved in the Community Associations Institute's California Legislative Action Committee (CAI-CLAC) as Public Relations Chair and has considerable expertise in California homeowner association law. She wrote and published *The Davis-Stirling Act in Plain English*, a reference work for association directors and managers on the primary body of law governing homeowner associations.

Ms. Grimm is accomplished in alternative dispute resolution and was involved in passage of Assembly Bill 55—the California ADR law. She serves as a volunteer mediator in programs providing low-cost mediation services and has represented individual homeowners and associations, privately assisting them in dispute resolution.

As part of her practice she helps common interest developments (CIDs) in updating their governing documents—CC&Rs, bylaws—and guides them through the often difficult approval process.

Ms. Grimm resides in the San Francisco Bay Area and practices community association law statewide.

Jim R. Lane

Jim Lane is an award-winning writer whose Ventura company, Streamline Publications, creates newsletters for home-owner associations and other businesses. His background includes serving as president of his condominium association for a period during which it was honored as a Community Associations Institute (CAI) Association of the Year one year and received honorable mention the next.

A retired military officer, Mr. Lane applied the principles of leadership, group harmony and personal recognition for volunteers to guide his 198-unit association successfully through complicated projects that included complete reroofing, a low-flush toilet retrofit, CC&R update and other significant projects. He applies this *in-the-trenches* experience as a director to his writing. Mr. Lane shares the techniques that have worked for him with others who face responsibility for their own associations.

He serves on the CAI Channel Islands Chapter Board of Directors and is delegate to the CAI California Legislative Action Committee. In this capacity he joins with Ms. Grimm and other volunteers from CAI chapters the length of California to introduce and monitor legislation that affects common interest development homeowners and their boards of directors.

Mr. Lane lives in Ventura and is a frequent contributor to CAI publications, the Ventura County Star and other newspaper Condo Corner columns. He serves as president of the Ventura County Writer's Club.

ORDER FORM

Send order form and payment (check or money order) to:
Beth A. Grimm, Esq.
3478 Buskirk Avenue, Suite 220
Pleasant Hill, CA 94523   Phone (510) 674-1500

The Davis-Stirling Act in Plain English $ 29.00/copy

_____ Number of copies $_____

    CA sales tax 8.25% ($2.39 each copy) $_____

    Shipping ($2.00 each copy) $_____

                            Sub total $_____

The California Homeowners Association
Legal Digest (annual subscription, 6 issues) $39.00/year

_____ Number of subscriptions $_____

    CA sales tax 8.25% ($3.22 each subscription) $_____

                            Sub total $_____

                 Total enclosed $_____

Send to (print clearly):
Contact Name: _____

Business/HOA Name: _____

Address: _____

City_____ State_____Zip_____

Phone (Optional)   (_____) _____

For multiple copies or subscriptions, include additional
addresses on a separate sheet.

ORDER FORM

FINDING THE KEY TO YOUR CASTLE
By Beth A. Grimm, Esq. and Jim R. Lane

Share your discovery with your neighbors. Every prospective owner, owner and resident of a condominium, townhouse or planned unit development property needs their own copy of *Finding the Key to Your Castle*. A perfect welcoming gift for new residents.

Finding the Key to Your Castle per copy price; $12.50 includes CA sales tax. (Orders of 25 or more copies, $10.50 ea—16% discount)

____ Number of copies @ $12.50 $ _____

____ Number of copies @ $10.50 (25 or more) $ _____

Shipping/Handling @ $3.50 per copy $ _____
($2.00 each—25 or more)

First Class Shipping add $2 per copy $ _____
($1.00 per copy, orders of 25 or more, single shipment)

                        Total enclosed $ _____

Ship to: Name _____
(PRINT CLEARLY)
           Address _____

           City _____ State____ Zip_____

      Phone (_____) _____

Send order form and payment to: Beth A. Grimm, Esq.
                                       3478 Buskirk Avenue, Suite 220
                                       Pleasant Hill, CA 94523
                                       Phone (510) 674-1500

ORDER FORM

FINDING THE KEY TO YOUR CASTLE
By Beth A. Grimm, Esq. and Jim R. Lane

Share your discovery with your neighbors. Every prospective owner, owner and resident of a condominium, townhouse or planned unit development property needs their own copy of *Finding the Key to Your Castle*. A perfect welcoming gift for new residents.

Finding the Key to Your Castle per copy price; $12.50 includes CA sales tax. (Orders of 25 or more copies, $10.50 ea—16% discount)

____ Number of copies @ $12.50 $ _____

____ Number of copies @ $10.50 (25 or more) $ _____

Shipping/Handling @ $3.50 per copy $ _____
($2.00 each—25 or more)

First Class Shipping add $2 per copy $ _____
($1.00 per copy, orders of 25 or more, single shipment)

                                   Total enclosed $ _____

Ship to: Name _____
(PRINT CLEARLY)
           Address _____

           City _____ State ____ Zip _____

       Phone (_____) _____

Send order form and payment to: Beth A. Grimm, Esq.
                                         3478 Buskirk Avenue, Suite 220
                                         Pleasant Hill, CA 94523
                                         Phone (510) 674-1500